THE JESUS TRIP

ADVENT OF THE JESUS FREAKS

THE JESUS TRIP

LOWELL D. STREIKER

ADVENT OF THE JESUS FREAKS

ABINGDON PRESS Nashville and New York

ISBN 0-687-20223-X
Library of Congress Catalog Card Number: 75-176324

Cover photo by Steve Sparks

Illustrations on pages 24, 26, 27, 64, 65, 70, 72, 76, 77, 80, 85,
87, 91, and 95 from *Right On.* Used by permission.

Illustrations and photographs on pages 21, 28, 29, 37, 39, 46,
47, 48, 50, 52, 71 (bottom), 88, 101, 105, 109, 113 (top), 119,
120, and 121 copyright © by *The Hollywood Free Paper,*
P. O. Box 1949, Hollywood, California 90028. Used by
permission.

Manufactured by
the Parthenon Press,
at Nashville, Tennessee,
United States of America

To Stephen and Susan

Contents

Introduction: Who Are the Jesus Freaks?

They are young. They are zealous. They look like hippies. They have turned on to Jesus. They are as fanatic for the gospel as they once were for drugs and sex.

They come in every shape, size, and color. They are "Jesus people"—Bible-toting, Bible-quoting, Jesus-praising, convert-making, sin-forsaking, noisy, forward, persistent pests for Jesus' sake.

To some observers the Jesus freaks are "a reproduction of New Testament Christianity." To others they are no more than a momentary teen-age craze. But one thing their friends and foes are agreed upon—the Jesus people may look like hippies with their long hair, faded work clothes, and fringed vests, but "at least they're not on drugs."

"At least they're not on drugs"—so says a nun in Milwaukee who criticizes their simplistic theology but respects their strict morality. "At least they're not on drugs," echoes a Jewish psychiatrist in Philadelphia who considers them an infantile escape from the problems of the real world but prefers them to the acid heads he has committed to the state hospital. "At least they're not on drugs," repeats a suburban Chicago mother deeply disappointed by her eighteen-year-old daughter's fanatic devotion to soul-winning activities but relieved that she is no longer experimenting with drugs and sex.

"Jesus is alive!" proclaim the Jesus freaks. "And

he is coming soon!'' Their lives have been changed. The old emptiness and boredom are gone. Having tried everything—drugs, sex, politics, materialism, Krishna consciousness, transcendental meditation, surfing, racing, and hippie communes—and found nothing, they have turned to Jesus.

They have left behind the everyday world with its insoluble problems. *Christ is the answer. Jesus is the key.* Why worry about racial strife, the polluted environment, the endless Asian war, the most serious economic slowdown since the depression? Jesus is the solution, or so say the Jesus freaks. ''Instead of boredom and despair, we have found peace, love, and joy. Instead of fear, we have hope. Insead of loneliness, we have a Friend.''

Once high on drugs, the Jesus freak is now high on Jesus. Jesus is the ultimate trip, a high which never ends. In the words of a former social dropout and heavy dope user, ''I asked Jesus Christ to take control. He gave me the inner peace I wanted and needed so badly. He gave me love for people I could not love on my own and a patience to endure the things happening around me. The emptiness I felt is gone. God has shown me that we have only to depend on Him.''

Who are the Jesus freaks? Most of them are former street people. What are street people? Hollywood evangelist Duane Pederson defines them as ''the thousands upon thousands of people who live on the streets. These people exist in abandoned buildings, on rooftops, in alleys, parks, on the beaches. And many live in VW buses. They have no other homes than the street.'' [1] To Hollywood alone over a million kids come each year from all parts of the country. They are dropouts, castoffs, and runaways, kids with only a sleeping bag and a second pair of Levis. As Arthur Blessitt, the ''minister of the Sunset Strip,'' describes his own congregation:

Most of them [are] under thirty—hoods, bikers, dopers, pushers, runaways, teeny-boppers, strippers, topless dancers, hippies, male and female

Photo by Steve Sparks

Arthur Blessitt

prostitutes, pimps, homosexuals, and two Syndicate soldiers who between them [have] committed five murders. They [are] a gaggle of unlikely interlopers, white and black, tie-and-suited, bearded and beaded, mini- and micro-skirted, blue-jeaned, leather-jacketed, turtlenecked, bare-footed, jack-booted, some unwashed, many . . . concealing acid, uppers, downers, chains, knives, and guns in their pockets and brassieres.[2]

How did the converted street people come to be called Jesus freaks and Jesus people? Duane Pederson explains:

Originally the press called us Jesus Freaks. On the street and within the Jesus Movement, the word "freak" isn't a bad word. A freak is someone who has gone to an extreme on anything—even Jesus Christ.

On the street, the word described the people who were dropping too much acid, or "speed"—or so much of something that they "freaked out." So they were called "acid freaks" or "speed freaks"—or some other kind of "freak," depending what they were "freaked out" on.

Basically it was speed, because that would really freak them out even more than acid. Acid is more of a head trip. But speed does something complete, something totally destructive to the person. A guy who's been a speed freak for a while gets "spaced out." His mind, or part of it, gets wiped out, destroyed.

One day as I was talking to one of the newsmen he said, "Those street people who get turned on for Jesus are freaks—'Jesus Freaks.'"

I said, "They're not freaks. They're people. They're Jesus People." Somehow the name stuck, and now the movement is called the Jesus People Movement.[3]

In writing this book why did I use the term Jesus freaks? For two reasons. First, not only did Duane coin the term Jesus people, but he has since registered it as a trademark. Second, "I'm another Jesus freak" remains a proud confession of members of

Photos by Scott Streiker

Photo by Sid Dorris

the Jesus movement. They in no way consider the expression derogatory.

What are my qualifications for writing about the Jesus people? *I was a Jesus freak!* That was over ten years ago, long before it was fashionable. I was saved at a Chicagoland Youth for Christ rally. I prayed for an hour daily; read the Bible through at least once a year; could quote Mark, John, and Romans by heart in the King James Version; witnessed to everyone I met; led a hundred souls to Christ; once distributed fifteen thousand gospel tracts in a single day; and gave my personal testimony more times than Babe Ruth hit home runs.

In my late teens and early twenties I served as assistant director for Chicagoland Youth for Christ, columnist for the Youth for Christ magazine, president of the Hi-Crusader Bible Clubs of Chicago, and editor at Moody Press (Moody Bible Institute). During my Philadelphia college years I was president of the Temple University chapter of Inter-Varsity Christian Fellowship, editor for *The Sunday School Times,* and student pastor of an inner-city church. These were happy years in many ways. (I met my wife at a

Hi-Crusader meeting which was held in the basement of the Salvation Army Building.) Although I am no longer the zealous young convert (and convert-maker) that I was in my teens, I am grateful that a world of experience was opened to me—a world which continues to fascinate me today and to which I have dedicated my life as teacher and scholar.

While still in college, I became a member of the Lutheran Church in America as a result of my appreciation of the liturgy of the Lutheran tradition, the writings of Martin Luther, and the Christian love shown to me and my family (our two children were born during my college years) by good people who happened to be Lutherans. Since earning my doctorate in religion at Princeton University, I have been teaching college courses dealing with the religious significance of contemporary life, particularly youth culture. My previous publications examine such recent phenomena as the hippies, the "religious ir-religion" of today's young people, drugs, the lure of Eastern religions, and the heroes of the counter-culture.

Earlier this year I co-produced and moderated a series of one-hour television programs probing current ethical and religious issues. It was during this time that distant rumblings of a revival of fundamentalism among the street people of California began to reach me. This book is a personal attempt to describe and interpret a significant religious movement. It is the record of impressions and reactions by one who is concerned with what he has observed. I have tried to be fair, to present persons and activities in as favorable a light as possible, and above all, to explain what is happening.

Based in California, the not-so-legitimate offspring of the perennial pietism of American Christendom, the Jesus freaks are on the march. Yesterday they seemed yet another manifestation of Hollywood fever—the miraculous appearance and instantaneous success of a superstar or superfad, which is here today and forgotten tomorrow. But today they are sweeping the country. Duane Pederson's tacky

Button
Courtesy The Hollywood Free Paper Emporium, *reproduced by permission.*
© Copyright 1971

Hollywood Free Paper, for example, boasts a circulation of over four hundred thousand and is reprinted in Kansas City, Detroit, Cleveland, Denver, Morrison (Illinois), and Worcester (Massachusetts). A directory of "Jesus Teach-ins and Raps" (Bible study and prayer meetings) lists activities in twenty-nine states, Canada, and Germany. A guide to "Jesus People Centers" (coffee houses, hotels, campus centers, job referral services, drug prevention help, and Christian night clubs) includes nearly 150 locations in California alone! Beachheads have been established by the Jesus movement in every part of the nation—in teeming cities and small towns,

SPARK

Photo by Steve Sparks
The Sacramento March, February, 1970

on college campuses and resort areas, along the Sunset Strip, and in the poshest Long Island suburbs. The Jesus people are on the air with broadcasts such as "Soul Talk" and "The Come-Alive Hour." They are in print with a myriad of newspapers which rival the underground press in number, circulation, ferocity, and crudity.

And tomorrow? Will they last? Should the Jesus freaks be taken seriously? Are we witnessing the dawn of the Age of *Agape* or the rapid growth and inevitable disappearance of the latest fad?

Before these questions can be answered, even more basic questions must be raised. Why do young

BLESSITT

WANTED:

JESUS CHRIST

ALIAS: THE MESSIAH, SON OF GOD, KING OF KINGS, LORD OF LORDS, PRINCE OF PEACE, ETC.

★ Notorious Leader of an underground liberation movement

★ Wanted for the following charges:

— Practicing medicine, wine-making and food distribution without a license.

— Interfering with businessmen in the Temple.

— Associating with known criminals, radicals, subversives, prostitutes, and street people.

— Claiming to have the authority to make people into God's children.

★ APPEARANCE: Typical hippie type — long hair, beard, robe, sandals, etc.

★ Hangs around slum areas, few rich friends, often sneaks out into the desert.

★ Has a group of disreputable followers, formerly known as "apostles," now called "freemen" (from his saying: "You will know the truth and the Truth will set you free.")

BEWARE — This man is extremely dangerous. His insidiously inflammatory message is particularly dangerous to young people who haven't been taught to ignore him yet. He changes men and claims to set them free.

WARNING: HE IS STILL AT LARGE!

Poster

Courtesy The Hollywood Free Paper Emporium, reproduced by permission.
© Copyright 1971

people become Jesus freaks? What is the principal attraction? Is the Jesus movement a good thing, or a very unhealthy development?

Rather than tell you what I think the answers are, I have decided to show you. For two weeks I lived among the Jesus freaks of California—the great mother lode of the movement. I attended their raps and services, lived in their communes and homes, went with them into the streets and college campuses, interviewed their leaders and more than a hundred of the kids, heard their petty squabbles and major disagreements, listened to them during hours of exuberance and moments of travail.

This is what I saw.

Tony and Sue Alamo's Christian Foundation

Certainly the most ecstatic organization I encountered among the Jesus people was Tony and Sue Alamo's Christian Foundation. It was a lovely cool evening after a scorching hot day when I drove to Saugus, nearly thirty miles north of Los Angeles. The area was hard hit by a recent earthquake. But even without the extensive evidence of the quake—fallen overpasses, condemned buildings, unearthed billboards—the region is remote and unappealing. The land is scruffy and barren, laced with steep foothills of hard, rocky soil. When the sun goes down, the countryside is as gaunt and lonely as the surface of the moon.

As I drove the Sierra highway, I wondered if I would ever find the abandoned restaurant the Alamos use as a house of worship and mess hall for their large Christian commune. In Los Angeles I had heard much about Tony and Sue—much of it unfavorable. The word was that they had been run out of L.A. by the police because they harrassed both residents and tourists with their immoderate "turn or burn" street preaching. I knew that they had inaugurated street witnessing and were largely responsible for the birth of the Jesus movement. But finding them seemed difficult. No one was sure where they had moved their operation. The best procedure seemed to be to allow them to find me, so I casually strolled Hollywood Avenue. Sure

20

enough, within a half-block four young zealots had approached me, eager to tell me how they had been saved and hopeful that I would attend a meeting that evening in Saugus.

"What are you doing in such a remote place?" I asked.

Their reply: "The Lord said that in these last days his disciples should flee from the city to the mountains."

My first sensation when I entered their testimony service was severe discomfort. All the doors and windows were closed, and the body heat of two hundred wildly gyrating bodies raised the room temperature to well over one hundred degrees. Here was an old-fashioned revival service with the beloved gospel songs ("What a Friend We Have in Jesus," "Amazing Grace," etc.), a ceaseless stream of personal testimonies (I counted forty), instrumental and vocal solos ("And now Sister Mary Jane will sing "In the Garden"), duets, trios, and a frenzied "Hallelujah Chorus" sung by the forty testimony givers (thus revealing that the spontaneity of the service was more apparent than real). Never have

ARE YOU HASSLED... BY THE DUDES WHO ALWAYS WANT TO "SAVE YOUR SOUL"? YOU KNOW, THE GUYS WHO ARE ALWAYS RAPPING ABOUT JESUS, TELLING EVERYONE THEY'VE GOT TO REPENT AND ALL THAT. WELL, DON'T WORRY, THEY WON'T BE AROUND MUCH LONGER... NONE OF THEM WILL BE ALLOWED IN HELL.

Illustration from The Hollywood Free Paper

Photos by Sid Dorris

I seen such energy, such fervor, such body-and-soul enthusiasm spent on religious worship. They were on the edge of hysteria the entire time. Arms lifted heavenward, feet stamping, all stops pulled, they screeched song lyrics unto God, moaned and groaned, shuddered, and had fits.

After the service I was escorted to the north Hollywood apartment of the Alamos, who were absent from the service. Tony and Sue sat warily at one side of a huge sofa. Sue is the heart of their operation, Tony the brains. She is late fortyish, hard-looking with crooked teeth and peroxided platinum hair. Tony seems younger, an aging crooner in Levis with a thickening waistline. They watched me like foxes until the ice was broken by the appearance of a busload of kids from Saugus. The occasion was a public unveiling of a phonograph record of the very music I had just heard at Saugus (including Sister Mary Jane's "In the Garden"). The ensuing scene

was a revelation. Tony and Sue are Mom and Dad.
They love each of these kids. And the kids love them
and do whatever Tony and Sue ask. And Tony and
Sue are no wishy-washy-do-as-you-please parents.
They are do-as-you're-told-or-else-get-out parents.
And for once in their lives these kids who have had
too much too soon, these kids no one has ever loved
enough to say no to, these advantaged kids from
broken homes, these aimless kids who don't know
what to do with themselves, these kids with too much
freedom, too many choices, and too little guidance—for once in their lives they have someone who
says, "These are the rules. Keep them and we'll love
you. Break them and we'll punish you."

"I'm sick of this sentimental slush about a God
of love," declared Tony. " 'God will understand. God
will forgive you.' What nonsense. God is a God of
wrath to those who disobey him and a God of love
to those who do his will and keep his commandments. And God says, 'Know ye not that the unright-
eous shall not inherit the kingdom of God? Be not
deceived: neither fornicators, nor idolators, nor
adulterers, . . . nor drunkards'—and that includes
every kind of drug addict—'shall inherit the kingdom
of God.' "

Tony and Sue Alamo are both Jewish Christians.

Cartoon from Right On

Their real name is Hoffman. Sue has been a Christian since childhood. After she was miraculously cured from a hopeless disease as a girl, her whole family was converted. But it was not until years later when she received the Pentecostal baptism of the Spirit and the gift of tongues that she began her ministry as a preacher. (And a frighteningly powerful preacher she is!) Tony was a vocalist and a recording industry executive when the Lord appeared to him in a vision right in the middle of a business conference and ordered Tony to inform his colleagues of His imminent return. (Both Tony and Arthur Blessitt state that Christ has appeared to them in person.)

Tony and Sue took to the streets five years ago. They have led thousands to "a saving knowledge of Jesus Christ." But the hippie appearance of their followers and their reputation for accosting tourists on the Sunset Strip with their "the world is coming to an end, repent or go to hell" urgency alienated the religious establishment and the Los Angeles police. More than once their meetings have been invaded by club-swinging police. On one occasion the police held the doors so that no one could leave the building and proceeded to lob mace into the interior.

Sue and I chatted for about thirty minutes while Tony and the kids consumed refreshments on the patio. I mostly listened to this outgoing, strong-willed lady preacher. Before I left, Sue invited me to return to Saugus on Sunday afternoon for interviews with her followers. I was flattered that she had offered. When I drove away, I noticed that the Alamo apartment was ringed with police cruisers. Were they expecting trouble? Were they monitoring the Alamos? Were they in the vicinity for some other reason? I never discovered.

I returned to Saugus on Sunday at one o'clock in the afterfoon. As I was explaining my purpose to the overseers—the title given to selected young people who have been with the Alamos for the longest periods of time (at least a year)—I noticed one

JESUS REJECTED BY TWO ORANGE COUNTY SHERIFFS

Illustration from Right On

of the young men lifting the telephone receiver. He was phoning the Alamos for clearance just as someone had done when I had made my earlier visit to Saugus. After I was O.K.'d, perspective interviewees began materializing one or two at a time.

"Tell me your story," I said to each of them.

Larry is a handsome guy with blue eyes and blonde hair. He is from Virginia. When Larry was a child, his father's assignments for the Pentagon kept him away from home for up to three years at a time. Larry was third in his high school class, but a month before he was to graduate (June, 1968), Larry dropped out. Thrown out by his mother, he went to Washington, D.C., and became a heavy drug user ("doper"). Finally bored by Washington's slums, he started traveling with a friend. As the result of several bad experiences along the way, Larry soured on mankind and decided to become a hermit. He was headed for Big Sur, where he intended to live alone in nature, when he hit L.A. He had been wandering aimlessly when he met a kid who offered him a free meal at a little church in Hollywood. There he met the Alamos and was saved. He has spent the past two years living at the Alamos' Foundation—praying, reading the Bible, and inviting others to attend services.

Kent is from upper New York state. His family has been active in the Episcopal Church for generations. A rebellious youngster, Kent was packed off to private prep schools, where he went from bad to worse. "I was pretty nuts when I was younger," he confesses with a grin. "I even shot myself once." He hated school and became involved in a SDS underground newspaper. "I didn't want to get an education so I started traveling. I was dealing drugs in Massachusetts." His interest in Far Eastern religions brought him to California, where he stumbled into a meeting. "All these kids were smiling, and their faces were glowing," he recalled. "I didn't know what they believed. I just knew they were genuine and happy. I started going to their services. Man,

Cartoon from Right On

they really irritated me—all this smiling. But then all at once I felt peaceful. I felt good. I went up to the altar and got saved. And then I wanted to go out and share what I had with everybody. Now all I do is pray, read the Bible, and witness. And I'm never bored. I'm satisfied. There's peace in my heart."

Greg is an intense, high-strung young fellow. He

has piercing brown-gray eyes, a moustache, and slim, narrow shoulders. He was born in Rochester, New York, but soon thereafter his mother inherited a large sum of money and moved the family to Spain. She divorced Greg's father, who was a minister, became a social climber, and finally married a BOAC executive. In his midteens, Greg was sent to boarding school in England, where he learned English for the first time. Curious about an America he had never known, Greg enlisted in the U.S. Navy. Completing his hitch, he toured the States. He reported: "I was surprised to see the corruption of this country. I was really shocked by what I saw—loose morals and poverty." He turned to drugs, especially hashish, bummed around Spain and Canada, and eventually headed for New York City, where he unsuccessfully tried to join the Merchant Marine. He drifted around Greenwich Village, experimented with LSD, wandered around the country, marched on the Pentagon, lived for a while in Boulder, Colorado, and drifted to Chicago, where he was arrested and charged with contributing to the sexual delinquincy of a minor. He spent months in Cook County Jail awaiting trial, beat the charge, and returned to New York, where he became hooked on "speed" (methamphetamine—a powerful stimulant). Sickened by his rapid degeneration, Greg headed for Florida, got a construction job, and cleaned himself up. "But I got bored," he recalled, "so I headed west—didn't even wait for my paycheck. I hopped a freight train for L.A. Wow! You wouldn't believe those freezing desert nights. When I got to L.A., I tried panhandling and was almost killed by a biker [a motorcyclist]. I became paranoid, confused," Greg paused for a moment.

"God put a thought in my head that Jesus is the light of the world," he blurted. "I just sat there for a long time. I was going to do what Jesus Christ did—the heaviest thing. But where was I going to get the power to do miracles like Jesus did? Just then someone gave me a gospel tract. I went to a meeting, and I felt the Spirit come into my heart.

Illustration from The Hollywood Free Paper

Then I knew where the power comes from. That was over two years ago."

While Greg was still talking, Tom had joined us. Tom has blonde hair and gray eyes and was wearing a sweatshirt with the number twenty-five emblazoned on it. Tom is from a Catholic ghetto neighborhood in the nation's capital. His mother divorced Tom's father and married a Marine. The family moved continually from base to base; his stepfather became an alcoholic; his parents fought incessantly. Many times his stepfather would load Tom's two half sisters in his car and go wildly careening around town. Tom never knew if he would see any of them alive again.

Illustration from the Hollywood Free Paper

As a high school student in Memphis, Tom and his friends went from beer to marijuana to pills. When his stepfather was sent to Camp Pendleton, Tom returned to Memphis to begin life on his own. After a few months he headed for California to join "the love and peace movement." "But instead of beautiful people, I found dopers and bikers and perversion and weird people." Tom recounted. "We had nightly drug parties. We were so stoned we didn't care about anything. We used to get busted, and we'd just laugh and laugh. The next day we'd be out of jail, and there would be plenty of drugs."

Tom continued, "Then my buddy Ed got saved through Tony and Sue, and he told me 'Jesus is coming.' Ed took me to Tony and Sue's. They pulled no punches—heaven or hell. So I got saved. Susie prayed me through. And right then I saw a vision of Jesus. But that was only the start. You've got to get grounded. They were closer to me than my mother or father ever could be. It was like I knew them all my life. I could trust them. They did the *whole* Bible. Not just the 'God is love' part. You know, 'No drunkards shall enter the kingdom of God.' " I knew.

Tony and Sue came to Tom's group—dopers, bikers, revolutionaries. Tom related: "Tony gave his testimony. And Susie preached a real powerful sermon. And all of them were saved. But some of them

didn't go the whole way. So Tony and Susie told them, 'If you don't want to serve God, good-bye.' And Tony and Sue took over the dopers' house right across from the Hollywood Presbyterian Church."

Tom went right on. "We started a twenty-four-hour prayer chain. Each of us puts in at least two one-hour shifts a day."

"What else do you do?" I asked. "I mean, do any of you work or raise crops or anything? After all, there are hundreds of kids living here at Saugus. Where does the food come from? It must cost hundreds of dollars a week."

"I don't know," Tom replied. "The Lord provides. You'll have to ask Tony and Sue. None of us work. We just witness." Tom thought for a moment and then he said, "If it hadn't been for Tony and Sue we'd all have ended up in a jail cell, on a morgue slab, or in a mental institution. That's all I know."

James, a young black from L.A., joined us. He had been about to graduate from high school in June, 1966, when the lure of the streets proved overwhelming. "I lived the fast life," he told me, "narcotics, hustling on the streets, for about three years. Two years ago, I was walking Sunset Boulevard when I got this gospel tract that said Jesus Christ is coming back to earth again. You know, it told about all those prophecies—vapors of smoke over the city, confusion on earth. Well, God sent out fear and conviction upon me. I went up to Tony after a service and asked him 'What must I do to be saved?' And Sue and Tony prayed me through."

Bumpersticker
Courtesy The Hollywood Free Paper Emporium, *reproduced by permission.*
© *Copyright 1971*

"Are you still in touch with your family?" I asked.
James nodded.

"What do they think?"

"My mother is glad I'm off the street," he answered.

Tony and Sue had entered the building. A crowd was forming for the three o'clock service, which was about to begin. Sue sat next to me and asked what I had discovered. I told her that I was impressed by their success with heavy drug users. It seemed to me that ninety percent of their kids were once

Poster
Courtesy The Hollywood Free Paper
Emporium, *reproduced by permission.*
© Copyright 1971

addicts. A look of disdain spread over Sue's counte-
nance as she gruffly announced: "Yes. Our kids
were dopers. Who else would take care of them?
If you O.D.'d [suffered a drug overdose] in church,
they'd have you arrested. You know what? There
is a revival going on. And every time there has been
a revival, the 'God is love' movement has moved
in. There's a revival going on, and all the resistance
is coming from the churches." Sue was preaching
at me. I had heard the same sermon at the Alamos'
apartment, but she was fascinating so I listened.
"It's always been the same story," she insisted. "The
churches and the establishment always stand in the
way. And you want to know why?"

I nodded, even though I felt I knew what she would
say.

"Money. That's why. The churches have too much
to lose. Look at the Bible. The Jews cried out to
God for a deliverer. When he came, they didn't like
his looks. So they crucified him. Now the churches
are crying out for revival. And God sent the hippies!
And they want to kill them."

Sue was gathering a full head of steam now. She
went on. "Revival—a move of God—has never come
through the churches. Look at Moses. He knew
nothing about the religion of the Jews. It was Aaron
that did. But Moses was raised as a Gentile. He was
a fugitive from justice because he had murdered
a man. But God used him. Look at John the Baptist.
'Repent,' he said. He dressed odd, so he offended
the establishment." Sue took a breath and con-
cluded, "Every prophet of God has been slain by
the churches and by the establishment." The service
had started. Tony was asking visitors to donate
copies of the Bible, "but only the King James Version, God's inspired Word." It was almost time for
Sue to preach. As Sue got up to leave, she motioned
to a tall, slim girl. "This is Cathy," Sue explained,
"our oldest and dearest convert. She's been with
us since the beginning. She's like a daughter to us.
Talk to her." And Sue was gone.

Cathy, one of the most attractive girls I have ever

Photos by Scott Streiker (above and bottom left) And Sid Dorris (bottom right)

seen, was apprehensive from the start of our conversation. I remembered her from my earlier visit to the Alamos' apartment. I had observed her washing Sue's dishes and looking after the Alamos' grandchild. Like a daughter indeed! A very rare daughter. Blonde, blue-eyed Cathy with the grace of a cat and the look of a lynx was one of fifteen children from a north California family. She had been on her own since she was fourteen. At eighteen she had come to Los Angeles for a job. She had worked as a dancer for three hundred dollars a week. Cathy seemed worried as she rapidly summarized her story. Not only was she saved through Tony and Sue, but five or six hundred of her friends had been converted also. "Five or six *hundred?*" I queried. "Uh-huh," she responded, nervously glancing over her shoulder.

"Do you plan to stay here forever?" I asked.

"What do you mean?" she said.

"Wouldn't you like to get married or—"

She interrupted. "I've got a husband somewhere. I don't even know where he is. I haven't seen him for years. Listen. I really can't talk to you now. Sue is going to preach and they really don't like us talking during services. I'll see you later." She slipped away.

I sat and wondered about Cathy and all the other kids at the Christian Foundation, all these attractive, joyful, personable youngsters. Something was bothering me. Why did they all seem eighteen years old? Why did I keep visualizing them in my mind as faultless specimens trapped in amber? Just because we find someone to love us, guide us, feed and house us, do we have to sacrifice our wills, our imaginations, our distinctive personalities? Does God want us to be personable teen-agers forever? All right, so Cathy and Larry and Kent and Greg and the rest have found a mother and father in Tony and Sue. But how long can they be Tony and Sue's perfect children? Five years? Ten years? Fifteen years?

Tony and Sue need not worry. As Tony remarked, "There are plenty of hippies for everyone. We'll never run out of kids. Who else wants them?"

JOIN·GOD'S FOREVER·FAMILY

What
Do
the
Jesus
Freaks
Believe?

The testimonies of the young people at the Alamos' *Christian Foundation* reveal the basic affirmations of all members of the Jesus movement. What do they believe? First the Jesus people believe that God has a simple plan of salvation. As Edward B. Fiske of the *New York Times* remarks: "The Jesus People are against social action and argue . . . that the way to change society is to change individuals." [4] In their conversations with unbelievers, their underground newspapers, the leaflets which they so promiscuously distribute, the placards which they carry and often wear, the Jesus people proclaim "four easy steps to God." The following is a composite drawn from innumerable examples.

Simple Steps to Salvation

Just as the universe is governed by physical laws which have been discovered by science, so is your relationship to God governed by spiritual laws which are found in the Bible:
1. God loves you and has a plan for your life.
John 3:16—"For God so loved the world, that he gave his only begotten Son, that whosoever believeth in him should not perish, but have everlasting life."
2. Sin separates you from God. Because you are sinful, you are cut off from God's love and his plan for your life.

35

Romans 3:23—"For all have sinned, and come short of the glory of God."

Romans 6:23—"For the wages of sin is death."

3. Jesus Christ died for your sins. He is your only way to God. Through him, you can experience God's love and his plan for you.

Romans 5:8—"But God shows his love for us in that while we were yet sinners Christ died for us." (RSV.)

John 14:6—"Jesus saith unto him, I am the way, the truth, and the life: no man cometh unto the Father, but by me."

4. You must ask Jesus Christ into your life as your Lord and personal Savior.

Revelation 3:20—"Behold, I stand at the door, and knock: if any man hear my voice, and open the door, I will come in to him."

John 1:12—"But as many as received him, to them gave he power to become the sons of God, even to them that believe on his name."

Romans 10:13—"For whosoever shall call upon the name of the Lord shall be saved."

At the center of your life is a God-sized void. Ask him to come into your life today.

Almost always a sample prayer is provided for the prospective convert. Again, I have constructed such a prayer from several examples:

Dear God, I know that I have sinned and that I need your forgiveness. I believe with all my heart that your Son, Jesus Christ, died for me.

Jesus, come into my heart as my personal Savior. Take away my sin and help me to follow you as Lord of my life.

I surrender my life to your control. Make me the kind of person you want me to be. Give me strength to tell others of you and to do your will in all areas of my daily life.

Thank you for answering my prayer. In Jesus' name. Amen.

But what does one do after he is saved? Again the answer is simple: read the Bible, pray, tell others about Jesus, join a Jesus movement group, and avoid sinning. Even the last requirement is easy to

fulfill, for to avoid sinning means no drugs, no sex outside of marriage, no hassling (heated argumentation), and no violence.

And that's all?

That's all. For the Jesus freaks take the Bible as a divinely inspired, inerrant, every-word-is-God's-message-to-me guidebook for all matters of faith and life. Totally ignorant of modern biblical scholarships and with a knowledge of the Bible which is often limited to a few favorite texts, the Jesus freaks hold the Bible to be literally true in every detail. Moreover, it is all that anyone need ever know, for the Bible supersedes the discoveries of biology, zoology, geology, psychology, history, and all other areas of human learning. With Jesus as a friend to whom I can always bring my problems and the Bible as an authoritative blueprint for life, what more does anyone require? So ask the Jesus people.[5]

But how do these thousands of kids support themselves?

God only knows! Some groups insist that their members engage in communal work—farming, cooking, housekeeping. Others operate small businesses which cater to the Jesus people: workshops which produce the posters, bumper stickers, pamphlets, and other movement artifacts; bookstores which sell the study materials and Bibles; bakeries; grocery stores; restaurants; and even a candle shop. The greater number merely "trust in the Lord," or so they say. In fact, they depend on the generosity of other Christians. One hears innumerable stories of how God supplied funds for an overdue rent payment, or an unpaid utility bill, or a check written without sufficient funds to cover it. What the Jesus freaks do not seem to realize is that their behavior borders on thievery. Also their manner of "trusting the Lord to provide" consists largely of informing as many straight Christians as possible of their extremity so that the Lord may "move" more fortunate (and hardworking) brothers to contribute to the nonworking brethren's support. Would it not be better for the Jesus freak to support himself as

JESUS POWER

REPENT·BOYCOTT HELL

ALL POWER THRU JESUS

Bumperstickers
Courtesy The Hollywood Free Paper Emporium, *reproduced by permission.*
© Copyright 1971

Photo courtesy Hollywood Free Paper, *Tom Jackson, staff photographer*

Charles Smith

even the apostle Paul and Jesus did? As Billy Graham insisted during his Second Chicago Crusade (June, 1971), Jesus "worked hard with his hands, and he was certainly not a dropout."

I gained an insight into the manner in which the Jesus people rely upon the Bible during an evening at Calvary Chapel in Costa Mesa (Orange County). Calvary Chapel is only three years old. During this short time its warm, soft-spoken minister, Charles Smith, has won teen-agers by the hundreds. A recent mass baptism at Pirate's Cove saw two thousand immersions. Young converts have been sent to over one hundred "Christian communes" up and down the West Coast. Song and praise services such as the one I attended are often so crowded that droves of teen-agers are turned away at the door.

The chapel is a huge air-conditioned structure that looks like a misplaced Disneyland pavilion which might be named "Zorro's Hacienda." The service was conducted by a toothy blonde lad named Ken

who annoyed me because he talked too much between the congregation's songs and because he
was ten times happier than the group, much like
a warm-up comedian.

An audience of neat, clean, and beaming high
schoolers with just a sprinkling of adults joined Ken
in a songfest which was prettier, more sedate, and
more modern than other services I attended in the
Los Angeles area. Many of the songs had a contemporary folk music sound instead of the gospel song
style I had heard so often before.

Ken M.C.'d the program, leading the singing and
introducing a pretty, guitar-toting, granny-dress-clad
soloist who performed selections of her own author-
ship (the lyrics were biblical quotations; the music
of most seemed identical), adding a frequent "Praise
the Lord!" and "Jesus is coming soon!" for flavor-
ing. After ominously reporting the activities of a
phantom hitchhiker who has been warning drivers,
including a "visiting Lutheran minister," of the impending return of Jesus and then disappearing without a trace, Ken launched into an impromptu dis-
course on the apostle Paul's advice on marriage
in I Corinthians 7. Ken's approach was all too typical
of the Jesus movement. "Trust in God. Wait pa-
tiently," he instructed his young hearers, "and God
will speak to you about the husband or wife he has
chosen for you." If you lack faith, you will only
receive "God's second best," that is, a Christian
who is not totally dedicated to the will of God. His
illustration was of a girl who knew that God wanted
her to marry a certain missionary. She waited seven
years for him while he served abroad but lost faith
and married another Christian ("God's second
best") on the very weekend that her intended returned. "If only she had waited on the Lord for one
more week," lamented Ken with ersatz agony in his
voice.

But what is this faith which determines every decision? According to Ken, "Faith is a sense of inner
peace." The Christian should do nothing but wait
until he has a deep inner assurance, and he will

Photos by Scott Streiker

know the will of God. Ken went on to say that the Bible forbids marriage between Christians and non-believers and even between dedicated Christians and a "backsliding partner." He maintained that divorce is justified in both cases. By citing "real situations" in which "God withheld his blessings" until both partners were right with God or a second-best marriage was dissolved, Ken advocated a submission to the emotions of the moment which can only be termed foolish and irresponsible. Such preaching is not biblical interpretation at all. It is not exegesis, the reading of meaning *out of* the text, but eisegesis, the reading of the interpreter's prejudices *into* the text. With few exceptions, Ken's technique was standard for the Jesus people.

Duane Pederson and the *Hollywood Free Paper*

I spent two afternoons at the office of the *Hollywood Free Paper,* the "underground" Christian paper which is distributed from coast to coast. I had to wait quite a while to see Duane Pederson, the paper's founder and editor. Duane is daily confronted by an endless stream of journalists, promoters, visiting evangelists, troubled street Christians, and alleged authors. As I was to find out several times during my two weeks in California, every big name in the Jesus movement is currently receiving star coverage from both the secular and religious mass media.

But Duane was worth the wait. He is a shy, handsome guy—a cross between Billy Graham and Paul Newman in appearance. He is quite Scandinavian looking with deep-set blue-gray eyes; a long, pointed nose; plump face; long sideburns; and a quick, engaging smile. He was wearing a T-shirt, chinos, boots, and a Mickey Mouse wristwatch. He is slightly round-shouldered and impressed me as a withdrawn, reticent man—hardly the mass-meeting evangelist I had pictured. He spoke slowly, deliberately—always watching my face for a reaction. "I had a terrible stammer as a child. I was a lonely, stuttering boy in Hastings, Minnesota." I believed him. "The thing I wanted most when I was younger was to make Christianity popular—as popular as I wished I were," he continued. He told me of how

Duane Pederson

he had decided to start an underground paper, of how it had grown from ten thousand copies an issue to 450 thousand. "I've made God a promise," he added, "that we'll hit a million by the end of 1971."

His dream had come true; this former night club magician and Bible school dropout (expelled for cheating) had made Christianity popular through the *Hollywood Free Paper* and by means of outdoor evangelistic services and Christian rock concerts. "I got letters from over six hundred people indicating that they had accepted Christ as the result of our first issue. And close to two thousand responded when we distributed the paper along the route of the Rose Bowl Parade."

Duane rocked in his swivel chair for a few seconds. "So we sow the seed by any means—by force, by compulsion, by fad. It doesn't make any difference—just so the seed is sown." Duane had anticipated the question of whether the movement was merely another fad. "Of course it's a fad," he went on. "In California being a Christian is the thing to do. But many are being swept in. So what if three weeks from now they're back on the street doing drugs, balling every chick in sight?" Duane launched into an exposition of the parable of the sower, which he obviously has used many times. "Jesus said that when we plant the good seed some of it will fall on fertile ground. And some will fall on stony ground. And some will fall on the street where the birds will eat it. And some will fall among thorns. So when I see kids get high on Jesus and then drift away, I don't get concerned. It only proves that the Scriptures are true." We continued to talk for almost an hour, and I sensed a terrible loneliness, an overpowering desire in the stuttering boy from Hastings, Minnesota, to be accepted and loved. I could not help but wonder what would happen to the *Hollywood Free Paper* and the rock concerts should Duane find someone who will love him as he so wants to be loved.

The next time I visited the *Free Paper* office, I was examining their many posters and bumper

Poster
Courtesy The Hollywood Free Paper Emporium, *reproduced by permission.*
© *Copyright 1971*

Cartoon Strip from The Hollywood Free Paper

stickers when Duane suddenly appeared in front of me with a photograph in his hands. "Hey, Lowell, what do you think of this? It's an idea for a poster." In the picture was Duane in his famous fringed leather vest. With him was a young couple. Duane had an arm benevolently placed around each of them. All three were knee-deep in water. "This is a couple that I married and then baptized," Duane explained. In my head I was asking who had given Duane the right to perform sacraments, but I only nodded as Duane spoke. "We'll put a Bible verse here." He pointed to the bottom of the photo. "You know, something like I Thessalonians 4:9: 'You yourselves have been taught by God to love one another.' "

Photo courtesy The Hollywood Free Paper, *Tom Jackson, staff photographer*

Ocean Baptism—Duane and New Christian

HOLLYWOOD
FREE PAPER

VOLUME 2   ISSUE 10

STRIKE FOR PEACE?

WHILE THEY ARE CHANTING...

PEACE — PEACE!

...THEN DESTRUCTION WILL COME ... AND THEY WILL NOT ESCAPE!

I THESSALONIANS 5:3.

THE OPRESSED MINORITY...

ALRIGHT CHRISTIAN, YOU'VE HAD YOUR 30 SECONDS OF FREE SPEECH, NOW BACK TO US, THE TRUE MINORITY!

STRIKE! FOR UNIVERSAL FREEDOM *

STOP THE WAR!

STRIKE FOR PEACE

STOP THE KILLING

STRIKE! FOR FREEDOM OF OPRESSED MINORITIES

DO IT

JUST BECAUSE YOU'VE SILENCED A MAN... YOU HAVEN'T CHANGED HIM

THIS WILL BE YOUR CHANCE TO TELL THE GOOD NEWS. MAKE UP YOUR MINDS AHEAD OF TIME NOT TO WORRY ABOUT HOW YOU WILL DEFEND YOURSELVES, FOR I WILL GIVE YOU SUCH WORDS THAT NONE OF YOUR ENEMIES WILL BE ABLE TO RESIST OR DENY WHAT YOU SAY. JESUS (LUKE 21:14-15)

CAL-STATE FREE SPEECH PLATFORM

* FREEDOM TO DO WHATEVER YOU WANT AS LONG AS YOU'RE NOT A CHRISTIAN, AND YOU AGREE WITH US...

CHRISTIAN LIFE FOR THE WORLD
BOX 1891 HOLLYWOOD CA 90028

Front page, The Hollywood Free Paper

"Uh-huh. It's a nice picture," I innocuously commented.

And exactly what is the *Hollywood Free Paper?* At first glance it is an "underground" newspaper like the *Los Angeles Free Press* or *Rolling Stone.* But on closer inspection it turns out to be a crude, overblown gospel tract. The contents are entirely predictable. The cover is usually an atrocious cartoon depicting the Judgment Day agonies of the condemned and the joys of the saved. The inside pages contain testimonies in hip clichés, ads for various religious publications, announcements of gospel rock concerts, and a directory of Jesus people groups, raps, communes, etc. Since the *Free Paper* is given away without charge, I do not doubt that Duane will keep his million copy issue promise to God. But I have visions of three hundred thousand copies being dumped in the Grand Canyon. Duane will not be concerned; he is sowing the seed, and as he related, more than one street kid has found Christ through a *Free Paper* he found in a gutter.

The
Children
of
God

Certainly the most controversial group is the "Children of God." This burgeoning and unwieldly operation is an outgrowth of the American Soul Clinic, Inc., a twenty-five-year-old "faith work" established by Fred Jordan to train Christian laymen to lead others to Christ. Soul Clinic now includes foreign missions, orphanages, skid row rescue missions, farms, schools, hospitals, and clinics throughout the world. In addition, a weekly worship service has been broadcast on a total of over eight hundred television stations.

The Children of God is a mushrooming movement with seven hundred young adults living in sixteen colonies in various parts of the country. I visited the headquarters of the movement, which are located in a grim warehouse in the skid row section of Los Angeles. The director of the Soul Clinic Youth Department, Freeman Rogers, a Southern Baptist preacher in his early fifties, was open and cooperative. He told me that the work was about two years old and had its greatest success among heavy drug users. He reported with a large measure of complaint in his voice that their converts "get as high on religion as they formerly got on drugs." As a result, there is a prevailing mood of fanaticism to the movement.

No one is accepted by the Children until he or

Cartoon from The Hollywood Free Paper

she is of legal age. Incoming members are required to sell all their possessions and donate the proceeds to the movement. They are given new, biblical names such as Sarah, Isaac, and Martha. All things are owned in common after the example of the Jerusalem church recorded in the book of Acts. The Children live a strict ascetic life in their Los Angeles dormitory and their various colonies: no drugs, no sex outside of marriage, and no outside work of any kind. All Children are fulltime Christian workers. Six hours a day are spent in Bible study, four hours in manual labor (the colonies are farms and ranches), and much of the remainder in witnessing, preaching the gospel on the streets.

The Children always travel in groups (because Jesus commanded his disciples to go in "twos and in threes" and also because the devil is less powerful over a group than over a single soul). They preach a straightforward "repent or go to hell" message and irritate other Christian groups by their insistence that only the Children are true Christians. Glossalalia, or speaking in tongues, is another hallmark of the Children. "Are you saved?" they ask people on the streets. If the passer-by answers affirmatively, he is next asked, "Have you received the Spirit?" or "Have you been baptized by the Spirit?" and finally "Do you speak in tongues?" Woe unto the Christian who indicates confusion or replies in the negative, for the Children assume that he has not been saved at all.

The Children are a suspicious and almost hostile lot. When I tried talking with them, I was subjected to a ruthless third-degree about my religious experience, baptism, vocation, and church attendance. I parried with a barrage of questions of my own, demanding to know the very same things about my interrogators. A truce ensued! They allowed me to be shown around and to meet several members even though the fact that I was not a "fulltime gospel worker" distressed them. I found former drug addicts, ex–drug dealers, a rock musician, and an unwed mother—all typical Children. They hardly say

Photo courtesy The Hollywood Free Paper, *Tom Jackson, staff photographer*

Children of God Building

anything other than Bible verses (out of context) and, "Hallelujah, Brother."

The normal procedure is to hold new disciples for about a month at the Los Angeles dormitory before sending them to one of the colonies. The word "hold" is none too strong, for there is an element of duress. Several instances were brought to my attention in which Christian young people were held against their wills for periods of as long as forty-eight hours, during which they were exhorted to give up all and join the Children. When such efforts failed, the recalcitrant were declared possessed of the devil and expelled from the premises. Homeless street people who turn to the Children for shelter are likewise excluded if they do not convert on the spot. Perhaps the Children have never read in the twenty-fifth chapter of Matthew: "Truly, I say to you, as you did it not to one of the least of these, you did it not to me" (vs. 45).

The Children of God is a community of obedience. By strictly obeying, by renouncing one's will, by giving up everything for the movement, the disciple finds purpose and fulfillment. As Freeman Rogers explained, "They become as radical for Christ as they once were for drugs, or sex, or the New Left." They are so radical in fact, that they reject all vocations except soul winning, all earthly ties, all secular involvements, all compromise with the world, all halfway methods—even those of the most conservative fundamentalists. "They are," says Rogers, "against all religion but for Christ."

All new disciples are required to take a three-month course of basic training. They are then eligible for three additional months of leadership training. After these six months of Bible study, disciples are encouraged to apply for licensing "to the gospel ministry" by the Soul Clinic. From what I could see, training consists of the faultless memorization of scattered verses from the King James Version of the Bible. Rogers was quick to point out that their understanding hardly equals their zeal. "They know the words, but they are unable to interpret them," he admitted. Here was but another instance of an indefensible fanaticism of which the adult officials of Soul Clinic disapproved but which they felt powerless to restrain. "I accept ninety percent of what goes on here [the Children's dormitories are in the same building as Rogers' office] and reject the rest." But so far the Soul Clinic's rejection has been unvoiced. After all, they have a good thing going. The Children of God figures prominently in their fundraising appeals and has brought them much favorable attention, for example, coverage on NBC's "First Tuesday."

Other Jesus people groups have turned against the Children of God. The *Hollywood Free Paper* printed "an open letter" from the Inter-Varsity Christian Fellowship of Southwestern College (Chula Vista, California) accusing the Children of God of invading their campus in order

Bumpersticker

Poster
Courtesy The Hollywood Free Paper Emporium, *reproduced by permission.* © Copyright 1971

to convince youth that their way is the right way, which includes the selling of all earthly possessions, following them as captives, held and taken somewhere in Los Angeles, taught *un-Christian Doc-*

trines, guarded at all times, with fearfulness shaking their bodies, no sleep, no food, and ignorant that Christ's Mission was to save man-kind from sin. After L.A., they are bussed to Arizona, taught in a hypnotical state, kept away from the sunlight, and filled with wickedness. These people pounce upon weak Christians, and pull them into an hypnotic state with their wicked eyes. These people are the "wicked forces of Satan" that produce fear, hate, greed and lust.

The adults taken from our campus have not been returned. Parents are concerned and broken hearted.

To all readers, please be on your guard. Have the guts to say, "With the blood of Jesus Christ and in His Name, Be gone ye follower of Satan." They will stare at the ground in shame. "Let no one deceive you, children!... The Son of God appeared for this very reason, to destroy the Devil's works." 1 John 3:7,8. [Today's English Version.]

Please get the word around, or either you or your friends' lives may be in serious spiritual danger.[6]

This warning was echoed at the JC Light and Power House by Jack Sparks of Christian World Liberation Front and by scores of individual Jesus people I encountered in Los Angeles and San Francisco. The most telling response was Tony Alamo's: "Children of God? Children of God? But we're all the children of God!"

Poster
Courtesy The Hollywood Free Paper Emporium, *reproduced by permission.*
© *Copyright 1971*

Are the Jesus People Fundamentalists?

The term fundamentalist came into vogue early in the twentieth century as a description of the conservative participants in the fundamentalist-modernist controversy. In 1895 a Bible conference at Niagara Falls drew up a statement of "fundamental" truths which separated "true Christians" from "modern apostates." These essential doctrines were: (1) the virgin birth of Jesus, (2) Christ's death on the cross as a payment for man's sins, (3) Christ's bodily resurrection; (4) the actual bodily return of Jesus to earth for the purpose of establishing the earthly kingdom of God, and (5) the absolute inerrancy of the Bible. *Every one of these doctrines is regarded essential by today's Jesus freaks.*

Fundamentalism was the child of American revivalism—the emotional religion of itinerant evangelists who reproved men for their sins, threatened them with divine wrath, and called them to sudden conversion at hectic meetings punctuated by the shrieking, trembling, and fainting of the repentant. Such revivals have swept America many times during our history. There was the Great Awakening of the eighteenth century, stirred by such evangelists as Jonathan Edwards, George Whitefield, and Gilbert Tennent; the camp meetings of the American frontier in the nineteenth century; and the modern mass evangelism of Dwight L. Moody, Billy Sunday, and in our own day, Billy Graham.

Revivalism with its pietistic individualism was firmly rooted in American religion during the early years of the republic. Direct access to God without the need for "externals"—priests, sacraments, liturgy, church organizations—suited the temperment of the rugged, self-sufficient individualists of the American frontier. As sociologist Bryan Wilson notes, "Salvation by individual decision to accept Christ fitted circumstances in which men had to decide things for themselves, without the strong social pressures of a settled social order. . . . Revivalism was suited to the atomised character of frontier society, and was one of the few agencies that could bring men together." [7]

But could such individualism cope with the complexities of modern life? Could the momentary excitement of a camp meeting conversion enable a man to deal with the rising price of manufactured goods, the collapse of farm produce prices, the problems of urban life, class struggle, labor disputes, riots, strikes, sweat shops, and alcoholism? For such were the problems of America in the late nineteenth and early twentieth centuries as immigration, industrialization, and urbanization transformed the character of our national existence.

How different from revivalism was the new Social Gospel, which insisted that the true Christian life was unselfish dedication to the improvement of society and its institutions. The Social Gospel movement was strongly influenced by Darwin's theory of evolution. The Bible was no longer regarded as a collection of infallible proof-texts providing authoritative guidance for all matters of faith and life. Instead the new biblical criticism treated the Scriptures as a record of an ongoing religious development, a collection of ancient writings which were better interpreted in light of the discoveries of archaeology, linguistics, and textual criticism than by an intuitive, devotional approach. The Bible was considered a record of man's progressive under-

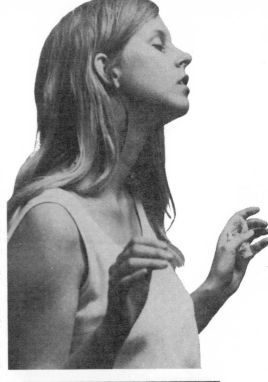

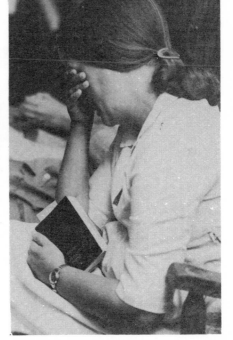

Photos by Sid Dorris

standing of God, not an inspired, inerrant revelation of an immutable diety.

The peace, prosperity, and technological progress of the early twentieth century seemed to confirm the Darwinism of the Christian liberals. Mankind was making perceptible progress. Little by little the world was getting better, and nothing could arrest its upward course.

Against such unwarranted optimism, such uncritical acceptance of the spirit of the age, the fundamentalist waged unrelenting warfare.

As conservative theologian Edward J. Carnell reports, orthodox scholars "sought to prove that modernism and Biblical Christianity were incompatible. In this way the fundamentalist movement preserved the faith once for all delivered to the saints." [8] Even liberal theologian L. Harold DeWolf praises the fundamentalists for their significant contributions to the life of the church. He declares:

> The fundamentalists continued a stress on Bible study and on the biblical message through times when the Bible was being widely neglected. . . . Insistence by the fundamentalists upon clarity and directness of theological affirmation was needed and is still needed. . . . The fundamentalists have stressed man's imperative need of God. . . . They have maintained the doctrine of a personal God, a Father with whom we can communicate in prayer, a Father purposively concerned with our human need.[9]

Also, they have focused attention on the person and work of Christ, and the urgency of personal decision for Christ. "Finally," states DeWolf, "the fundamentalists have cultivated among millions of Americans the practical piety of earnest personal prayer, world-wide evangelical concern, generous giving, and warm Christian fellowship." [10]

In earlier periods revivalism had encouraged a highly individualized, emotional, and anti-intellectual approach to religion. It reinvigorated established churches and led to the creation of Sunday schools and home and foreign mission societies, as well as colleges and seminaries for the training of Christian ministers. But it also introduced a spirit of dissension which constantly divided the church. Since revivalism was more concerned with sincere feelings than clearly articulated theology or orderly ecclesiastical polity, it often produced a restlessness of spirit which bordered on anarchy. Rapidly recruited converts, whose religious knowledge was limited to a few intense hours of experience, were loathe to settle down in the established congregations of traditional denominations. They distrusted traditional creeds, formalized worship, theological discussion, or anything else which might distract Christians from their major responsibility: the conversion of sinners.

A basic weakness has always afflicted revivalism. Since it is easier to recognize and condemn the errors of established institutions than to establish positive alternatives, the revivalist has found it simpler to attack his enemies—real or imagined— than to deal creatively with society and its problems. Church historian Jerald C. Brauer declares: "Revivalism tended to ignore . . . basic questions as it concentrated on one great problem: Are you saved? In so doing it helped to promote Christian faith in America, but at the same time it de-emphasized the role of the Church by concentrating on an individual experience, and it also made Christianity a stranger to large segments of American intellectual, cultural, and political life." [11]

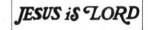

Bumperstickers
Courtesy The Hollywood Free Paper Emporium, *reproduced by permission.*
© *Copyright 1971*

The essential negativity of revivalism is most apparent in its understanding of morality. A good man is one who *refrains from* behavior such as smoking, drinking, social dancing, and cardplaying. As long as a man *avoids* these temptations, he is considered righteous in the eyes of community of born-again Christians. The result is a negative or cultic ethic, more concerned with status in the religious ingroup than responsibilities to one's neighbor. While placing great emphasis on condemning trivial social practices, revivalistic Christians have been generally unconcerned with major social issues.

Photo by Steve Sparks

"One Way"

The fundamentalists, the twentieth-century descendants of the revivalistic heritage, have fallen prey to the same weaknesses. Originally a movement of protest against modernism, fundamentalism has become essentially an attitude of dogmatic intolerance and intractable resistance to denominational Christianity. According to Carnell, "Fundamentalism made one capital mistake. This is why it converted from a religious movement to a religious mentality. Unlike the Continental Reformers and the English dissenters, the fundamentalists failed to develop an affirmative world view." [12]

The negativity of fundamentalism caused it to lose much of its influence in the period between the two world wars. In recent years it has shown renewed vigor, calling the confused and frightened to the comfort of the unchanging gospel. The most successful fundamentalist undertaking has been the mass evangelistic crusades of Billy Graham. Almost as significant are the large number of youth-oriented evangelistic organizations—such as Youth for Christ (co-founded by Graham and now known as "Campus Life"), Campus Crusade for Christ, and Inter-Varsity Christian Fellowship—which have sprung up in the past quarter-century. Dogmatically fundamentalistic and thoroughly revivalistic, these movements spread like wildfire in the late forties and early fifties, waned in the late fifties and during the sixties, and have shown a renewed vigor in recent months particularly among the Jesus people. Indeed, it is difficult to decide whether the evangelistic groups are responsible for the Jesus movement or the Jesus movement is responsible for the resurrection of the evangelistic groups!

It should be noted that the same period which produced the Jesus people has witnessed the zenith in the career of Billy Graham. Never has the prestige or popularity of a revivalistic evangelist soared to such heights. Exceeded in the admiration of his fellow citizens only by the President (and, according to some polls, the Vice-President), Graham is today the virtual chaplain of mainstream America. Ironi-

cally, it cannot be said that Graham or revivalistic Christianity has achieved any significant influence upon our present national life. Once a dynamic force which transformed the churches and energized social reform, revivalism today seems to provide temporary emotional comfort for those confused by a chaotic and rapidly changing world without in any way challenging the churches to renewal or prophetic social concern. Perhaps the Christian faith is no longer what so many Christians think it to be—the primary formative influence which shapes the attitudes and aspirations of the American people.

As we have seen, when it comes to the "fundamentals" of the faith, the Jesus people are definitely fundamentalists. But they differ in at least one vital respect. They are willing to abandon the sins of their former lives but not their youth-culture lifestyle—hence the hippie appearance which many conservative Christians find reprehensible.

Photos by Scott Streiker

It is not unusual for people to turn to the truths of an earlier, simpler time when they are confronted by insoluble personal and social problems. The same nostalgic quest for their more innocent youth sends thousands to Laurel and Hardy film revivals and fills a Broadway theater for performances of *No, No, Nanette.* Many fall back upon the religion of an earlier, less urban, less chaotic, less threatening America. Like all nostalgia, the return to revivalism is a romantic search for a time that never was. It is a momentary emotional release from the demands of a world which changes too rapidly, requires too much. At fundamentalist evangelistic services one finds large numbers of adults on the brink of middle age dressed as if it were still the 1950s and they were still courting. Their hairstyles, clothes, and demeanor are twenty years out of style. The impression is that such audiences have stopped the clock, have rejected the world of the sixties and seventies—a world in which patriotism is derided, sexual taboos are ignored, good manners are forgotten, traditional values are assaulted, national leaders are assassinated, hard work is despised, acquisitiveness is condemned; a world without "inferior" racial and social groups in terms of which one can proclaim one's superiority; a world where it is not even necessary for one's body and clothes to be spotlessly, odorlessly, antiseptically clean!

Indeed, who chooses to live in such a society at such a time? I certainly do not. Who wants to give his children such a world? Not I. But the problems of today do not disappear because we flee to the comforts of yesterday. A man or woman can dress like a child for a hundred years, but time is not deceived. No matter how tightly one clings to the pretense of youth, the unavoidable conquerors are coming—sickness, grief, age, and death.

The Jesus movement does not seek this kind of return to a more tranquil past. It *is* an escapism of sorts—of that there can be no doubt. But it does not bind itself to middle class, middle American, pre-1960 morals and manners as does much fun-

JESUS IS LIGHT

Illustration from Right On

damentalist evangelism. The Jesus movement is a *youth* phenomenon grounded firmly in the generation gap, counter-culture thinking which has been popularized (and commercialized) by television, movies, the press, and popular literature for the past four or five years. The Jesus people owe much to the fundamentalism of the past. Their doctrines, evangelistic methods, and understanding of the Christian life are not so much New Testament Christian as American revivalistic. But their style is all their own—part converted hippie, part redeemed drug scene, part the strange world of today's youth, part anti-establishment.

As I see it, the Jesus people occupy the territory between adult society and the anti-adult counter-culture. The Jesus movement rejects both the establishment's love of material goods, toleration of injustice, and mindless disregard for the quality of life and the counter-culture's adoption of violence, drugs, sexual promiscuity, and whatever else their parents find offensive.

Wherever the Jesus people find that a given institution is uncritically pro-establishment, they will have nothing to do with it. On this count most religious organizations, mainline denominational and fundamentalist, are rejected, and for their part, such established religious groups have nothing but contempt and hostility for the long-haired, hippie-like Jesus freaks. But wherever a group is discovered that shares the Jesus movement's sense of "in the world but not of the world" identity, the Jesus freaks are among its friends.

Illustration from Right On

From what I have seen, I must judge that the Jesus movement is essentially sectarian, that is, world denying, intolerant, exclusivistic, authoritarian. The only religious groups with which it feels at home are such sects as "independent" fundamentalist churches, nondenominational gospel chapels, and such relatively loose-knit sectarian fellowships as the Assemblies of God. And all too often the Jesus freaks are rebuffed by even these groups because of their beards, beads, and casual dress.

Photo by Steve Sparks

When it comes to the conservative denominations (e.g. the Reformed churches, the Southern Baptists, the Missouri Synod Lutherans, and the various Presbyterian splinter groups), there is ill-disguised distrust on both sides. Although the conservative denominations of today are the sects of yesterday, they have made their peace with secular society. As sociologists of religion have demonstrated, "If the sect is defined rigorously, it cannot last beyond the founding generation. Family life, increasing wealth and respectability, and routinization [the development of organization, structure, and standards for the training and selection of leaders] with the passage of time lead to accommodation by the sect." [13] Thus most sects have become churches within forty years of their inception. Ironically, it is the reaction of conservative denominations to the Jesus freaks which reveals that they have almost completed this transition themselves.

Some fundamentalists welcome the Jesus people as a healthy and desirable outpouring of the Spirit.

Billy Graham claims that the Jesus movement is "sweeping the country. It doesn't bother me that it might be a fad. At least it is a positive fad. I'm for anything that promotes the gospel of Jesus Christ." Floyd L. McClung, a Church of God minister from Tennessee, found them "clean and neat and radiant with the love of Christ." (One wonders if it is necessary to be "clean and neat" in order to be "radiant with the love of Christ.") Such openness is often prompted by a belief that the Jesus people are potential members for present fundamentalist sects. Perhaps this is so. But what if the Jesus movement is radically different from earlier forms of revivalism? What if it is a completely new Christian life style? Will fundamentalists continue to befriend the Jesus people should they prove totally unassimilable?

But why are the Jesus people unenthusiastic about established fundamentalist groups? Precisely because they are established—organized, routinized, calm and orderly institutions of an adult world for which the Jesus people are not yet ready. "Where do you go to church?" I asked pretty young Jan at a Bible rap. "I don't go to church. I come here," was her reply. The generation gap yawns again! To an eighteen-year-old Jesus freak even the piety of the fundamentalist independents is too staid, too dogmatic, too intellectual for his supercharged, hyperactive, turned-on generation. And as for Billy Graham, the Jesus freaks believe that he has sold out to the establishment. "Do you know what Graham said?" one kid asked me. "He said that Richard Nixon is one of the greatest men he's ever known. And Richard Nixon doesn't even believe in Jesus. He may be a great man, but if he doesn't believe in Jesus, he's going to hell. Has Billy Graham ever told *that* to Richard Nixon?" The Jesus people will undoubtedly support Graham's forthcoming Oakland Crusade because it provides them with an opportunity to "do their thing," which is soul-winning. But the "Chaplain of the American Establishment" they can do without.

Forty
Private
Jesus
Trips:
The JC
Light and
Power House

My most disappointing experience was with the JC Light and Power House, a "Christian commune" near the UCLA campus in Westwood. Founded about two years ago by evangelists Bill Counts and Hal Lindsey (who make only occasional appearances at the House like the Lone Ranger and Tonto), JC Light and Power House is a Christian training establishment and dormitory for forty residents. In addition, the attractive and spacious mansion is the scene of weekly Bible "raps" (study hours) and occasional "schools" (retreats) conducted by the staff and visiting luminaries.

The Light and Power House was my dwelling place during my first five days in L.A. I had opportunity to interview several members of the staff as well as many of the residents.

My favorites were Mike, Kevin, Jim, and Trudy.

Mike is the house manager. He is a tall, handsome, athletic fellow in his midtwenties. He sings well, is a capable counselor, and is bright. In fact, he has so many gifts that they bewilder him. Mike is totally confused about his future. The months are slipping away on him as he considers professional football, show business, graduate school (psychology), and fulltime Christian service.

Kevin is a physical culturalist with wall-to-wall muscles. He handles the gardening and all the heavy physical work at the house. And what a superb gardener he is! It is really touching to see this lug of a guy bending tenderly over his flowers.

Jim is the house cook—a mountain of a boy with an explosive sense of humor, a good mind, and a kind heart. And he knows his sauces and spices!

Trudy is a pretty brunette, about twenty-four. She seems stand-offish, remote at first meeting—an impression which prevents many people from getting to know her. I liked Trudy because she is a striver. She sets goals and pursues them, which is all too rare among the Jesus people. But she too was in the throes of indecision when I visited the Light and Power House. She had resigned an excellent job in Los Angeles and was thinking of returning to Grace Haven Ranch in Mansfield, Ohio, where she once had been responsible for the daily care of twenty-four people. She seemed a girl who could be touched, could be hurt, had been hurt, but was willing to risk it all again. A person who has been hurt badly in the past learns self-protection, thus her apparent coolness. Trudy did not spill her religious autobiography to me the way virtually every other kid did when they found out I was a writer. How refreshing! She is also the only Jesus people (the term is used as a singular as well as a plural) who has written me since my return from California. "My greatest hope," she says, "is that your book will be a glorious witness for the Lord." She reminds me of Gandhi's advice to Christian missionaries: "Don't talk about Christianity. The rose doesn't have to propagate its perfume. It just gives it forth, and people are drawn to it. Don't talk about it. Live it. And people will come to see the source of your power."

With the good company of Mike, Kevin, Jim, and Trudy, why was my stay at the Light and Power House so disappointing? The disappointment came because the Light and Power House is forty kids each on his or her own separate Jesus-and-me trip. I have never encountered such utter disregard for the rights of the community or the needs of one's neighbor. Serious emotional disturbances are ig-

• BE MY ONE AND ONLY,
• BE MY ONE AND ONLY,
• JESUS
• BE MY ONE AND ONLY
• FRIEND.

Cartoon from Right On

Photo by Steve Sparks

Bill Counts

Photo courtesy The Hollywood Free Paper, *Tom Jackson, staff photographer*

Hal Lindsey

Ad from Right On

nored or "left to the Lord." The community's food supply is regularly raided at midnight, leaving nothing for breakfast the next morning. Appointments are broken without explanation (three of the kids failed to show after they offered to accompany me to other activities; one left me stranded in Sherman Oaks), the right to privacy is disregarded, and to put it bluntly, no one seems to give a damn about the other residents. One blistering hot day Jim and Kevin toiled for hours building a concrete and brick planter around a large tree in the front yard. Three of the boys walked right through the wet cement despite Kevin's protestations.

The kids I interviewed fell into two categories. First there were the college kids who regarded the house as a bargain dormitory. Second there were the "fugitives," girls between the ages of nineteen and thirty who were using the house as a refuge from life. For example, I met a nurse from Hawaii who spends each day in her room and the basement tape room (where a collection of casette recordings by Hal are available but rarely used). She has spent so little time in the light of day that I took her for an albino! She has a private phone (everyone else uses a single coin phone in the lobby), her own TV, and is seldom seen by the other residents. When I talked with her, she indicated sheer disgust for normal boy-girl relations with "all this hand-holding, arm-around-the-waist, kissy-facey familiarity."

Another gal, a sweet-looking blonde from north California is always on the verge of tears because of imaginary romantic and financial problems. The fact is that she has a fiancé waiting for her in the East but is terrified at the prospect of making such a forever-and-ever commitment.

Such kids drift into and out of the house at a fantastic rate. Kevin estimates that over a hundred have lived there in the past year.

I got a taste of their Christian training program at a Wednesday night Bible rap. The house was packed with more than two hundred visitors, most of them in their late teens or early twenties. Mike started things off by leading a few songs such as "He Lives!" and "How Great Thou Art." He was as effervescent as usual. "It's really *neat* to have a relationship with Jesus!" he spouted.

I had picked Hal Lindsey out of the crowd. You can always tell who the leader is. He is ten years older than anybody else, and he wears the wildest shirt. So it was with Hal. He came on strong like a used-car salesman. He was excitedly waving a magazine. "How many of you have seen this week's *Time* magazine?" he asked. "Let's have a clap for Jesus. This *really* is a *really* fair coverage of what *really* is happening." (Hal's every other word is "really." Apparently he thinks his hearer doubts him.)

Hal then launched into his favorite topic: the impending return of Jesus. His text was Daniel 9:24-27, in Hal's words, "one of the most startling and fantastic prophecies in the Bible." I must say the manner in which he pulled time fixes out of the text, piled up obscure verses from both testaments completely out of context, invented meanings for the verb tenses of the "original" Hebrew, uncovered hidden calendars, and adduced irrelevant archaeological evidence was indeed "startling and fantastic." But his finest performance was his negation of all the world's ills and woes. "When the Lord returns, there will be no war, there will be no racial strife, there will be no poverty or hunger, there will be no air pollution. Jesus is *really* gonna get it together." What a superb rationalization for ignoring the duties of Christian citizenship in a perplexing world and a frightening age! Leave it to Jesus.

Bumpersticker
Courtesy The Hollywood Free Paper Emporium, *reproduced by permission.*
© *Copyright 1971*

Hal personifies the "Jesus is coming soon" fervor of the entire Jesus movement. Everything is seen as a fulfillment of prophecy—the Arab-Israeli conflict, air pollution, the recent California earthquake, X-rated movies. Even the fact that I am a Jewish-Christian was cited as evidence. As I was told *ad naseum,* my faith is proof that the Lord is "gathering his ancient people unto himself." Several Jesus people were upset when I told them that hundreds of thousands of Jews had joined the

churches during the second half of the nineteenth
century. California's few hundred Jewish Jesus
freaks are a drop in the bucket.

As I listened to Hal, it struck me that everything
a given group teaches its followers about the Bible
and the Christian life can be learned in one evening.
The essentials are always the same: "You are a
sinner. Jesus died for you. God will forgive you if
you accept Jesus as your personal savior. The Bible
is the inspired Word of God. Read the Bible, pray,
and tell others of God's saving love." And that's
it. All the rest—Bible prophecy, tongues, and the
many tiny differences which divide the various segments of the Jesus movement—are less important.
But even these are simple matters which can be
presented in about an hour.

I guess I have been a Christian too long. Perhaps
if I had examined myself and my faith less, I would

Baptisms in the Sproul Plaza Fountain

know more. The Jesus people know so much. But then the average Jesus freak has "been in the Lord" only a month or so. And the average "fulltime Christian worker" has been a Christian for about three months. As my mother-in-law warned me when I left for graduate school, "The more you know, the more you know that you don't know." If Jesus does not come soon, there are going to be thousands of not-so-confident former hippies. *Really.*

Particularly distressing to me is the Jesus movement's emphasis on the imminence of Christ's return. "Jesus is coming—soon. The only literature I need in order to interpret the Bible is a daily newspaper. A biblical prophecy about the Second Coming is fulfilled on every page." This is what more than one Jesus freak declared. Before long the "rapture" will occur. "Jesus will descend with a trumpet's blast, and all the redeemed will rise to

Illustration from Right On

meet him in the air. Then the Great Tribulation will follow. Satan and his human allies, the Russian hordes, will war against God's ancient people, the nation Israel. Things will go pretty bad for the tiny nation. But just when things look blackest, Jesus the Messiah will descend on the Mount of Olives and rescue his people.'' And with the return of the King and the destruction of his enemies a thousand-year rule of peace shall begin—so runs the fundamentalist scenario adopted by the Jesus freaks.

''What will you do this fall?'' I asked Danny, a converted Jew who helps out at the *Hollywood Free Paper.* Danny stared at me with bewilderment in his eyes. ''I mean, will you be going to college or working?'' I explained. He shook his head and answered, ''Hey, man, don't you know the Lord is coming?''

"But what if he doesn't? What if Jesus tarries? After all, this isn't the first time Christians have believed that the end was at hand." But Danny has an infallible timetable. I could not budge him.

Emphasis on the imminence of Christ's return has always had paradoxical repercussions. Some Christians are inspired by this doctrine to an earnest dedication of their lives to the Christian gospel. After all, "Only one life, 'twill soon be past. Only what's done for Christ will last." But others use the impending end of the age as an excuse to cop out, to abandon responsibilities and discipline. Earlier in this century, observes Allan H. Sager,

> many fundamentalists declared that indeed a glorious future was sure to come, but that it would come through the arbitrary stroke of God, not through the struggles of men to realize illusive social ideals. They shared the belief that the world was essentially evil and that not only would it remain so but would grow more so until God himself finally destroyed it. Indeed, the logic of this position pushed to the conclusion that the worse the world got, the more reason for hope in the imminent Second Coming.[14]

Thus, the church is seen not as an agency for the amelioration of human misery but as an ark through which a select number of righteous souls will be saved in the impending cataclysm. The world is lost. Prepare to leave. Such is the message of the Jesus freaks.

If the Jesus people had any sense of Christian history, they would know that sects which stress millennialism rapidly lose their influence, for when the awaited advent fails to materialize, the fervor of the group cannot be sustained. As Bryan Wilson says, such sects are "often of relatively brief duration, or, in becoming institutionalized, undergo a change in their response to the world."[15] With few exceptions they have never attained sufficient stability of organization to endure for any great length of time.

Illustration from Right On

The Jesus freaks view the world and everything in it—mankind in particular—as radically evil. If they are right, then all human efforts are doomed to futility. If this is so, why should a man strive to overcome evil in his society or in his own heart?

Surely, I think, this is a counsel of despair. All that God has created is good. It becomes evil only when it is abused. Man is called to share with God the ongoing work of perfecting all things, of fulfilling all creative potentialities. In this task God and man are partners, not enemies. So I believe, despite the voices of the Jesus people. The choice is between *godliness* and *godlikeness,* between a religiosity which abandons the world to its unfathomable perversity and a partnership in the sufferings of the God who woos all things to a consummation and fulfillment which they persistently resist. In the end each man must decide whether it is better to save himself or to refuse to escape into a private salvation until the entire world of one's responsibilities has been brought to fulfillment.

Why Do They Become Jesus Freaks?

Our young adults by tens of thousands have turned to the Jesus movement—why? What kinds of families do the Jesus freaks come from? What burdens has adult America placed on the present younger generation? What are the major crises of adolescence in America? What is conversion, and how is it related to adolescence?

What Kind of Families Do They Come From?

Many of the Jesus freaks are from broken or unhappy homes. Some are from the major urban ghettoes. Some are from very wealthy families. But for the most part the parents of the Jesus people are "middle Americans—hardworking, average income, "one home in the suburbs, two cars in the driveway, summer at the seashore" Americans. They believe in God, send their children to Sunday school, occasionally attend church themselves, worry about property values, taxes, and layoffs at the plant.

Above all, the parents of the Jesus people believe in "the American way of life"—the importance of the family, the need to work hard in order to obtain the benefits of the "good life," the sanctity of private property, the freedom to pursue comfort, security, and pleasure. What enormous economic strides these parents have made in the past four decades!

But, alas, the dream has become a nightmare; for the United States of America, the strongest and wealthiest nation in the history of mankind, is a land of poisoned air and polluted water, of racial strife and rampant crime, of personal instability and interpersonal alienation, of ulcers and divorce. The parents of the Jesus freaks are beset by skyrocketing expectations, hopeless dreams, and insatiable appetites; for the foundation of their lives is the advertiser's hollow promises of eternal youth, instant success, and sexual irresistability—all for the price of a pack of cigarettes, a tube of toothpaste, an aerosol can of deodorant, or a bottle of mouthwash.

The Children of the Dream

And what of the children of the American dream—the well-fed, well-housed, well-schooled makers of our tomorrow and disturbers of our today? The late Robert F. Kennedy heaped accolades upon them. "Not since the founding of the Republic," he declared, "has there been a younger generation of Americans brighter, better educated, more highly motivated than this one." He praised them for "an idealism and a devotion to country matched in few nations, and excelled in none." In his inaugural address, President Nixon echoed this sentiment: "We see the hope of tomorrow in the youth of today. I know America's youth. I believe in them. We can be proud that they are better educated, more committed, more passionately driven by conscience than any generation in our history."

Yet implicit in these celebrations of the passion and idealism of today's younger generation is the recognition that the usually stable, albeit tense, relationship between the young and their elders has been severely shaken. The young find themselves alienated from their parents' world and value structure. Today's adults have been radically "de-authoritized" in the eyes of their sons and daughters. In the words of one observer:

America has lost no wars; it has suffered no depressions. The generation of the fathers has achieved an unbroken chain of material successes for almost thirty years. If the failure is neither *military* nor *economic*, we can only conclude that it is essentially *moral*. Listen to the voices of the students. They accuse the fathers of the very crimes that the fathers lay at the door of Nazi Germany and Communist Russia: racism, genocide, imperialism, aggression, authoritarian manipulation of subject populations for selfish and evil ends.[16]

The Burden of Youth

What is wrong with our young people? Why do they reject our values, our attitudes, our way of life?

In order to answer these questions it is necessary to understand what it is like to be a young adult in contemporary America. Before the modern industrial age, children passed almost directly into adulthood. Shortly after puberty, a young adult left the strict control of his parents in order to assume the full responsibilities of adulthood: earning a living, establishing a home, pursuing lifelong goals, and rearing children of his own. The concept of a "between age" characterized by extreme emotionalism, a separate culture, distinctive apparel and manners, and even a private language is practically an invention of twentieth century America. The tendency to regard this period as normal is a result of the extension of education (more than half of our young people are now in college) and the manner in which Americans glorify youth, attempting to linger in it as long as possible (witness grandmothers in miniskirts and grandfathers in Italian sports cars!). As French historian Philippe Aries observes, "Our society has passed from a period which was ignorant of adolescence to a period in which adolescence is the favorite age."

We have come to accept prolonged adolescence, an interlude of many years between childhood and adult life, as necessary and even desirable. Accord-

Photo by Scott Streiker

ing to William Braden of the *Chicago Sun-Times,* we assume that "adolescence is a restless and romantic period that all young people must inevitably experience: a time of rebellion against authority, of philosophical perplexities, of flowering idealism, of conflict and struggle." And the length of adolescence grows and grows. For America's affluence is based on our expanding technology. Technology, in turn, depends on special skills, and such skills require more and more education. Thus the period of preparation for adulthood is steadily increased, and entrance into the adult world is incessantly postponed. In addition, our technological society requires ever larger numbers of highly skilled technicians but ever decreasing numbers of unskilled or generally trained individuals. Thus those young people who do not attend college, those who drop out of college, and even most of those who graduate from college (especially those with liberal arts degrees) face poor prospects for the future.

Photo by Sid Dorris

The majority of young people react to the moratorium on adulthood with patience and good humor. Having no power to change their lives, they turn to their separate culture for identity, comfort, and direction. Since they are imprisoned in the present, they seek all that their present stage of life offers. Some pursue "kicks"—speed, sex, drugs, random acts of violence and vandalism. But as psychologist Kenneth Keniston notes, "Most college students seek milder forms of experience: good times, girl friends, fun with the gang, the exploration of nature, happy days in summer, even art, music, and poetry. The American myth of 'carefree college days' is dominated by an eternal present where things are done just for the fun of it." [17] Society tolerates a breathing space, an opportunity to experiment, to play roles, to assume identities which may be retained forever or discarded in an instant.

But how carefree are the adolescent years? For some teen-agers they are happy, almost totally blissful. In later years they will be recalled with fondness and nostalgia. But for others the teen-age years are excruciatingly painful—years of confusion, anxiety, and alienation.

No longer children and not yet adults, many young people become totally estranged from the society which forces them to wait endlessly for admission. Dissatisfied with their state and powerless to change it, they direct their rage at their parents and all adult-controlled institutions. Some try to change the society against which they harbor such resentment. Others reject that society as beyond redemption, choosing to drop out and seek some private salvation through drugs, oriental religion, or life on a rural commune. Some adopt what psychiatrist Erik Erikson terms "a negative identity," rejecting everything which their parents taught them to value and valuing everything their parents taught them to reject. Most float from one immediate satisfaction to the next with no fixed direction or goal. All too often a mood of depression, apathy, and indifference settles upon them.

And many become converts.

Crisis Conversion

Sudden conversion—the emotion-charged passage from one plane of existence to another—is a normal adolescent phenomenon (if anything adolescent may be termed "normal"). As the teen-ager stands on the brink of adulthood, he becomes painfully aware of his incompleteness and imperfection. In consequence he broods, becomes morbidly introspective, is attacked by depression and anxiety, and feels sinful and guilty, as if he had transgressed some unknown moral law. A hundred new urges disturb him. A thousand new voices demand his attention. A thousand possibilities present themselves to him, leaving him confused and bewildered.

The adolescent struggles after a sense of identity, agonizes after a hopeful direction for his future. He

Cartoon strip from Right On

TRUTH

FUNNIES

"COMPARATIVE RELIGIONS IN A NUTSHELL"

not just in his teachings, or his moral code, but in his whole person, Christ is the source, sum and essence of every partial form of truth ever expressed or envisioned by any man: "for it is in him, and in him alone, that men will find all the treasures of wisdom and knowlede" ... "all of human history shall be summed up in Christ, everything that exists in heaven or earth shall find its perfection and fulfillment in him." (col. 2:3; eph. 1:9 ~ phillips)

Jesus says: " I am the way and the truth and the life ... every man who loves truth recognizes my voice"

Religious tract

is on his own, neither his elders nor his peers can solve his dilemma for him. With every passing year the pressures mount, the need to choose becomes more unavoidable, the present appears more terrifying. Considering the paucity of emotional support the young receive from their elders, who both envy and despise them, and the temptations to which they are exposed (drugs, sexual permissiveness, the boredom-spurred violence of the campus and the ghetto), it is a wonder so many survive with reasonably whole skins or psyches and find a place for themselves in adult life.

Some find answers. Some do not. Many cling to solutions which suffice for the moment but which prove in a matter of weeks to be only passing fads. The causes come and go—civil rights, the peace movement, communes, Eastern religions, ecology. And all too often the brightest, the gentlest, the most sincere seekers are left disillusioned, incapable of committing themselves to anything or anyone.

There is in all of us a hunger for something absolute, for something worthy of our unconditional devotion, for something in which we can believe and which, in turn, will transform our lives. For all of us are discontent with ourselves: tired of our failures, dissatisfied with our limitations, sick to death of our weaknesses. Most of us have learned to live with ourselves, to excuse our transgressions, to accept our foibles. But the young find all possibilities limitless, all decisions matters of life or death. And when the strain becomes too great, the self-dissatisfied young person does not try to make peace with himself but rather to escape from himself. He finds a better or ideal state of existence. He falls in love. Or he finds a movement to which he can sacrifice himself. Or he is born again.

Illustration from Right On

Religious conversion, romantic love, and enthusiasm for a cause are identical in this respect: they offer an opportunity for the individual to lose his limited self through union with a greater reality. The ardor of the religious convert, the dedication of the zealot, and the rapture of the lover release a flood of feelings which sweep away doubts and despair. As Theodor Reik observed: "An irresistible power from within seems to govern and lead the recipient, floating through him and carrying him beyond himself." [18]

The Jesus freaks manifest one such response. During the past few years I have met converts who were every bit as zealous on behalf of drug-induced mysticism, astrology, or Krishna consciousness as the Jesus freaks are on behalf of Christ. The pattern is always the same: (1) radical self-dissatisfaction grows into a sense of cosmic discontent (don't we all say, "Life is rotten," when we mean, "I feel rotten"?); (2) the socially acceptable solutions to one's personal dilemmas fail to work; (3) solutions which are condemned by society as a whole but advocated by one's fellow malcontents prove even more worthless than the socially accepted answers; (4) a mood of quiet despair prevails; (5) suddenly through a flash of insight everything falls in place, the malcontent finds *the* answer, and his life is transformed.

I mentioned above that many Jesus people are converts from the counter-culture. The major evangelistic efforts of the Jesus movement are directed toward hippies, "heads" (drug users), and New Left radicals—and in large measure these efforts have been successful (except for the New Leftists, whose "revolutionary" life-style represents a conversion of a very different sort). No Jesus people "Free Concert" (a euphemism for an evangelistic rally) is complete without a complement of ex-junkies and former street people. But the greatest success of the Jesus movement is not as a replacement for the counter-culture but as a viable life-style for those who are totally repelled by the street life whether they formerly wallowed in it or not. The form of the Jesus movement—its jargon and outward appearance—may be counter-culture, but its content is the "you must be born again, have you found Jesus as your personal Savior? Jesus Christ is the only answer" brand of fundamentalism.

Illustration from The Hollywood Free Paper

The Jesus people are not as much counter-culture as counter-counter-culture. There is much that is wrong with the world—war, racism, exploitation of man by man, moral corruption, environmental pollution, the insensitivity of men to their neighbor's needs. On this the counter-culture and the Jesus freaks are in complete accord. But on the causes of such problems and the nature of their remedy, these two groups of young people part company. The root of our problems is not Vietnam, nor the economic exploitation of our minorities, nor sexual repression, nor male chauvinism, nor the bomb, nor our inability to express our feelings and touch one another. The sole cause is our rebellion against God. So say the Jesus people. And the answer is not neo-isolationism, nor socialism, nor communes, nor free love, nor drugs, nor women's liberation, nor sensitivity training, nor chanting *"Hare Krishna."* The one and only answer is Jesus Christ.

Simple? Deceptively simple? Or perhaps just too simple?

Bumpersticker
Courtesy The Hollywood Free Paper
Emporium, *reproduced by permission.*
© Copyright 1971

"Like a Mighty Army": Christian World Liberation Front

After a week in Los Angeles I flew to the San Francisco area to look into the activities of the Christian World Liberation Front. CWLF is a loose-knit confederation of "ministries" headed by "Daddy" Jack Sparks, a former statistics professor from Pennsylvania State University. A few years ago Jack gave up teaching to work with Campus Crusade for Christ in San Bernardino, California. In 1969 he felt led to Berkeley as a missionary to vast hordes of street people who roam the vicinity of the University of California campus.

Jack began inviting kids to worship services at his home. As needy youngsters turned on to Jesus and off to drugs, Jack invited them to live with his family. Soon the Sparks home became a Christian commune—the first of dozens, which now dot the Bay. (A lawsuit brought by neighbors who objected to the impromptu meetings and the presence of the long-haired youth forced the disbanding of the first commune.)

I took a cab from the Oakland airport to a ratty, rundown building in a hostile black section of Berkeley which houses CWLF. My work-ethic sensibilities were effronted by the squalor of the furnishings and the fact that at two in the afternoon my arrival awoke some of the residents. I should have left such sentiments in Philadelphia. Steve Sparks,

Bumpersticker
Courtesy The Hollywood Free Paper
Emporium, *reproduced by permission.*
© Copyright 1971

Jack's teen-age son, showed me around the premises, which include a print shop where CWLF materials are churned out; a storeroom stacked high with movement paraphernalia—the gray workclothes which are the standard CWLF uniform, sweatshirts and T-shirts covered with movement slogans ("I'm Another Jesus Freak," "Jesus Power," and "One Way"), buttons (*"Agape,"* "God Is Dad," "Rap with God," "God's Love Is Warm"), bumper stickers ("Super Soul Shepherd: Jesus," "If you hear a trumpet blast, grab the wheel. The driver of this car is saved," "God's Speed Doesn't Kill"), psychedelic religious posters (CWLF's "Wanted: Jesus Christ" has become a Jesus movement classic), pamphlets ("Letters to Street Christians"—hip paraphrases of the New Testament Epistles—and "People's Medical Handbook," which explains how to eat a balanced diet for seventy-nine cents a day, how to detect venereal disease, the effects produced by various drugs, and how to attain mental health by "knowing Jesus and talking with him"; and accounts of such movement heroes as street evangelist "Holy Hubert"), a tiny office furnished with orange crates and discarded furniture; and yet another storeroom filled with back issues of CWLF's newspaper, *Right On.*

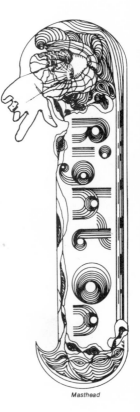

I had asked Steve if he could find someone with a car who would be willing to run me around to the various CWLF activities—raps, communes, street preaching. I offered to pay fifteen dollars a day plus gas and meals. Just as we were conversing about the matter, Brother Hector Ortega happened on the scene. Since he was the only person there who owned an automobile, I repeated my offer to him. In a few seconds I had not only a guide but a host. Hector insisted that I stay with him and Charlotte, his bride of two months, at their nearby apartment. "We have a spare bedroom—my wife's sister stays with us, but she's gone for the summer," he stated. "And we could sure use the bread."

After I got my belongings squared away and had dinner with the Ortegas, the three of us headed for the Monday night Bible rap held in a barnlike struc-

Masthead

Photo by Theo Kann, Berkeley, California
Brother and Sister Ortega

ture near the university. Fifty kids were distributed around the room, most of them seated on the floor. Jack was in charge. He is a rather funny-looking guy of about medium height and slight build with a broken nose and hair that recedes in front but hangs down to his shoulders in the back. He was wearing Levis; a washed-out, knit, mock-turtleneck shirt; and new construction boots—in sum, an acceptable CWLF uniform. His speech exhibited a studied attempt to be colloquial, to sound "with it." I took him for another of these middle-aged teenagers I have met in so many Christian groups. After all, here was a forty-one-year-old man with a Ph.D. in psychological statistics who dressed like a hippie and dropped the "g" every time he used a word ending in "ing."

I was also bothered by the dynamics of the group, or should I say the lack thereof? Here were fifty kids soaking up Jack's every word without criticism or

Photo by Steve Sparks
Jack Sparks

Photo by Steve Sparks

CWLF Monday Night Fellowship Meeting

discussion. After a few opening hymns and numerous announcements, the rap meandered aimlessly along. Jack had the group read aloud a few verses from Galatians. "Do you get the gist of what Brother Paul is talking about in this chapter?" he asked rhetorically. A long silence ensued. Finally a black kid came up with a fine interpretation of the passage. Jack treated him disdainfully. "No. That's not what Paul means," he pontificated. The black kid tried to defend his view, but a fat kid sided with Jack and further humiliated him. Arnie, a super-sensitive Jewish boy from New York took a crack at the passage. His explanation was logical, well reasoned, and well presented, but he was totally frozen out by the group—no one as much as looked at him. Then Jack smugly announced, "Just in case you want to know. Just in case it matters," and he gave an edifying little talk interrupted only by cries of "far out" and "right on" (the Jesus people's versions of "amen").

Masthead

Photo by Steve Sparks
CWLF Meeting

Finishing his homily, Jack lashed out at the Children of God group, which had begun to invade CWLF turf. Jack reduced their doctrine and life-style to a caricature at which everyone laughed, termed them "unscriptural" and "of the devil," and encouraged the group to join in the verbal assault. An unlovely we-are-holier-than-they session followed. The general verdict was that you can tell whether another group is "of the Lord" by the "vibes" you receive when you talk to them on the street. One girl proudly pronounced: "I met some of them and I got bad vibes. That proves they're not of God." As she was saying this, I was receiving even stronger negative sensations about her, which demonstrates how dependable "vibes" are as a test of truth.

Jack requested a hymn. Before it was sung, he carefully explained the full significance of the lyrics lest anyone should miss it. Then he took a collection with the words: "Let's pass the hat. If you have money to spare, you put it in. If you need some, take it out." (The house lost, every piece of paper money disappeared as quickly as it was donated. Most of the change followed.)

I talked with a number of the CWLF regulars at the rap that night and in the days that followed and came up with a few generalizations about their audience. The typical Jesus people meeting (Bible rap, prayer meeting, praise service, or whatever) attracts an average of twenty-five kids. Boys always outnumber girls by a ratio of five to three. This was the case in Los Angeles as well as San Francisco and held true whether the audience numbered five or five hundred. There are few college students in the movement but many high school and college dropouts. There is little achievement orientation. Few hold jobs or desire to hold them. Most of the Jesus freaks live in groups of three or four, some in larger communes of various sizes. They sleep until noon, read their Bibles and pray for a few hours, and spend the remainder of their waking hours as self-styled Christian workers—distributing tracts and newspapers, engaging other street people in conversation in an attempt to lead the unsaved to Christ, and starting public arguments with other organized freaks such as the Krishna Consciousness Society (an Indian religious cult whose members can be recognized by their saffron robes, shaved heads, and incessant outdoor chanting). Most of the CWLFers and their counterparts in Los Angeles are from broken or unhappy homes, have been alienated from their families since their midteens, claim to have had a serious drug problem before their conversions, and are totally turned off by the materialism, loneliness, and boredom of straight society.

Tuesday night found us on the back steps of the Berkeley Student Union building for another Bible rap. Again Jack was in charge. (He later complained to me that he was running himself ragged because of the unreliability or overinvolvement of the other staffers. I reminded him that even Moses had learned how to delegate authority.) This session was more a riff than a rap. The subject was the imminence of Christ's return. A fat fellow insisted that the Lord would be returning at any moment. "So many signs are being fulfilled: wars and rumors of wars, air pollution, the return of the Jews to their homeland—" Jack cut in with one of the sanest remarks I heard in California, "Look, every age has seen the events of its time as the fulfillment of prophecy. Let me put it this way: let's say that there are seven conditions mentioned in scripture which have to be fulfilled before the Lord comes. In every age since the time of the early church at least four of them have been fulfilled and three left unfulfilled. Maybe it's the same today."

"But the Lord could come next week," the fat brother persisted.

"Sure," said Jack, his patience wearing thin. "He could come tomorrow or right this minute for that matter. But you know it's easy for Christians to get into a prophecy trip and to ignore the rest of their responsibilities. I've seen it happen plenty of times." ("Right on!" I mused.)

Most of the leadership of the Jesus movement is pitifully uneducated. Duane Pederson is a Bible-school dropout; Arthur Blessitt could not make it through college; Tony Alamo was a recording industry executive. They will probably lose much of their following when their converts begin asking questions which they cannot answer. But as for Jack who knows better, has been a Christian longer than the rest, who realizes that Jesus may not return for years, I wonder. It may be that on the already overburdened shoulders of this one man rests the future of the whole movement.

Photo by Ed Mullen from Turned on to Jesus, Hawthorne Books, Inc., © copyright 1971. Used by permission

Arthur Blessitt

Photo by Steve Sparks
Duane Pederson

Photo by Steve Sparks
CWLF Leaders, l. to r., Billy Squires, Jack Sparks, and Ken (Koala Bear) Winkle

CWLF Headquarters in Berkeley

At Jack's suggestion I toured some of the area Christian communes with Hector. Our first stop was in nearby Richmond, where five brothers live in a small bungalow. Seth and Pete told me how they were saved, the problems they were having with their neighbors and the local police because of their long hair, and the difficulties of living together. People would stop them on the street and ask, "Why don't you get a haircut?" Their reply: "What's the difference whether my hair is long or short? I'm changed on the inside. That's what counts." But the police did not see it that way. From time to time they barged in looking for drugs.

A local doctor had opened a hundred dollar a month charge account for them at a local grocery store. Everything else was provided "by the Lord." "Do any of you hold jobs?" I asked.

"Not regular jobs," Pete responded. "Sometimes we pull weeds or things like that. You know, odd jobs."

Their major problem was a lack of direction. Seth explained, "The oldest Christian here has only been in the Lord for a year. We really don't know what to do, how to organize, what to study, how to spend our time. So we hitch into Berkeley and witness a lot." And that very afternoon I saw them distributing *Right On* at the Berkeley campus.

The Ortegas and I had returned for an afternoon Bible rap allegedly on the subject "Radicalism and the Bible." A local Evangelical Covenant pastor was in charge. First he embarrassed us all with apologies for looking "so straight." "At least I've let my sideburns grow a little (heh, heh)," he alibied. "I'd grow my hair longer, but my wife won't let me (heh, heh)." The kids squirmed. His exposition was purely devotional, Sunday morning sermon stuff. The kids hated it. He was supposed to be presenting the radicalism of the Old Testament. Instead he took each of the Ten Commandments, categorized it according to some exaggerated scheme of his own devising, and made a few pious applications. His ignorance of the Mosaic Law, the history of the Hebrew nation, and the development of Jewish interpretation of the Law was abysmal. He proceeded to congratulate himself for having publicly chastised area clergymen for their social involvements, especially opposition to the Vietnamese War. "Why can't they realize," he elocuted, "that the war is only a symptom? The real problem is *sin*. Until man's nature is changed, it makes no sense to deal with specific problems." Normally this approach would have brought several shouts of "far out" and "right on," for this sort of "convert enough men and all problems will disappear" simplism is what every Jesus people leader espouses. But for once the kids sensed that this was a cop-out rather than a solution.

Cartoon from The Hollywood Free Paper

The pastor's closing thought was, "If I'm ever lost in a barren wilderness, I intend to depend on the finest survival manual ever written. Do you know what that is?"

"The Bible?" several kids offered.

"The book of Leviticus," the preacher answered. "It's still the best book on hygiene around. It tells you what to eat and what foods to avoid."

"Nonsense," I broke in. "That's not how the Law

PEOPLES MEDICAL HANDBOOK

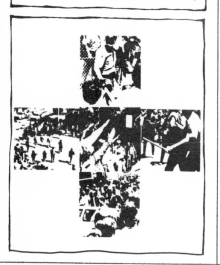

Raisins are inexpensive and satisfy a yen for sweets as well as being nutritious.

Bread should be high protein — look on the labels. Go to the day-old bakery thrift shops if you can. The spread should be the special margarines made with safflower or corn oil. Regular margarines are made from saturated oils and also have less nutritional value. The special margarines are soft and are sold in small plastic containers. Butter is expensive and besides most skin rash in young people can be traced to too much butter fat.

Getting CALORIES

Carbohydrates are the usual sources of calories in a diet: bread, potatoes, rice, beans, spaghetti, etc. Most people who don't have much money for food get too many carbohydrates. The trouble is that they tend to load onto the body as fat. All fat and overweight people have a problem here. The carbohydrates are digested rapidly and tend to go to fat unless the person is physically active. Watch your weight and look at yourself — if you are putting on weight, cut down on carbohydrates.

The simplest carbohydrate food and one of the most tasty is a baked potato. One easy way to cook them is to wrap them in aluminum foil. Eat the whole potato, skin and all, with salt, pepper, and margarine to taste.

Eggs are cheap! They can be eaten raw

in milk — with a little sugar and vinegar they taste like a milk shake. They are easily boiled, soft or hard, and they can be fried for plate eating or sandwiches. Eggs are a rich source of important nutritional elements.

Do not buy hot dogs, bacon, ham, pork, or luncheon meats. All of these are extremely high in animal fat, and they have little nutritional value. Always buy lean meat. If you buy ground meat, you will need to watch to be certain that you are not buying ground fat. Most of us can chew tough meat. It is just as nutritious and a lot less expensive.

Oils are very important in the diet. The best oil is vegetable oil from safflower, corn or cotton seed. Coconut oil and chocolate are saturated fats and you should avoid them along with butter fat. Vegetable oils have a real advantage in low cost eating because they are absorbed slowly from the intestines and satisfy hunger for many hours after eating. These oils will not cause weight gain and they will protect from skin rash and acne.

Soups?

Most soups, especially the commercial ones, are not high in calories or other food values. Bean and Pea soups are exceptions to this rule. By the way, beans, peas, and lentils are outstandingly nutritious foods if you cook them yourselves from the dried seeds with salt and onions. They are also most inexpensive.

---

has new beauty. About 10-15 percent of all trips are BAD DOWN TRIPS. A lot of people have killed themselves on bum trips.

There are few physical side effects that are immediately noticeable (unless you do something violent to yourself while on a trip). Studies have shown some more far-reaching effects however. Some people report flash backs several days or even weeks after taking acid. There is also evidence of damage to reproductive cells. Your children could be affected and after continued use it has been found to result in loss of memory.

There are several of these and more keep popping up: Bennies, dexies, whites, pep pills, etc.

People who take these say they feel more alert and more cheerful. Some people get jumpy and suspicious. Those who shoot these drugs often have hallucinations and get fanciful ideas about what is going on around them. It is easy to get dependent and most people have to keep increasing the dose to get a high. High blood pressure and malnutrition from a lack of desire to eat are common.

Common downers are reds, yellow jackets, goof balls, etc. Most are capsules, some are tablets. A few people shoot the powder dissolved.

These drugs help people relax and are often used as sleeping pills. They relax you and make you willing to do things you would not ordinarily do. You tend to like people better and see things as funny under moderate dosage. Heavy doses make people gloomy and quarrelsome. The effects are really a lot like those you get from alcohol.

There is a real danger of taking too much and dying. Also, people get hooked on these drugs and then if they can't get them their bodies really react with shakes and fits and hallucinations — real bummer. Some people die in this state. Mixing these with alcohol is an absolute no-no.

Most speed comes as crystal dissolved into a liquid. People sniff it, but most people mainline it. The result is a real active high. Sexual interest sometimes increases, sometimes decreases.

This is really a heavy drug. There are signs around which say "Speed kills," it does. People on it forget about eating or taking care of themselves. Eventually there is noticeable damage of the brain. It rots your teeth and multiple infections come to those who mainline speed.

HEROIN

The first two or three times you use smack you usually get sick, then high. The problem is that your body soon gets dependent on it. After that, all you get is a reduction in tension and relief. Most people who use it for a while get hooked this way. There are a lot of complications. Since most people who use

heroin mainline it, there are a lot of people who get sick and die from infections. Many forget about food and poor health results.

The strength of the heroin sold varies a lot. It runs from 5% heroin to 80%. Most is about 20%, but you never know. The result is that each year about 1% of all addicts die from overdose.

PEYOTE & MESCALINE

The peyote buttons are bitter and make you very sick. But they do produce hallucinations if you take enough. Mescaline is a powder refined from the buttons. It is more pleasant. The chief problems are what you do to yourself or others while on a trip.

INJURIES

We live in a time of frequent violent confrontations in the streets. You can get hurt whether you are an active participant or not. If you spend much time in the street or student culture, you are bound to come across people sometimes who are injured and need help. We can't tell you here all you need to know about taking care of injured people, but if you follow the basic principles, you can usually help.

With an injured person the first things you should check, unless they are obvious, are the breathing and the beating of the heart. Next is bleeding. You should learn how to give mouth-to-mouth resuscitation and heart massage. Anyone can learn these with practice.

Bleeding generally needs to be stopped, but don't be panicked by what looks like a lot of blood. Profuse bleeding can usually be stopped by firm direct pressure over the bleeding area for about 10 minutes. Get the

injured person to help. This calms him and helps prevent shock.

Shock can be very dangerous. The person gets cold and pale and his heart beats very fast. Treat him confidently and keep him warm. Find a doctor as quickly as you can, but don't run off and leave a person who is in danger of shock.

Most of the gas being used in street confrontations is CN tear gas. Sometimes the stronger CS gas is used. They cause nausea and burning. Don't rub your eyes blink them a lot, but get to water and wash them as soon as you can. If you get a lot on your skin, wipe it off with mineral oil or alcohol.

Mace, which really isn't a gas but a liquid spray, is also used sometimes. It is worse than the other two and needs the same kind of treatment.

BULLET WOUNDS

These are really scary and dangerous. Stop external bleeding and get the injured to a doctor.

The People's Medical Handbook, *a self-help booklet published,* by Christian Revolutionary Medical Committees

works at all. The Jews were under a covenant which set them apart from all the other nations as a peculiar people. Why, there are kosher foods that abound with infections and forbidden foods that are harmless. Chicken is kosher although it harbors a host of diseases while a goat kid that is cooked in its mother's milk is not. Do you know of anyone who has ever died from goat meat cooked in goat's milk?''

"Well, it's very interesting to hear your opinion (heh, heh)," the pastor stated. "You've obviously given a lot of thought to these things."

A wild-eyed Coast Guardsman waved his Bible at me. He had done the same thing the night before on the steps of the Student Union. "And what would you do if you were lost in a wilderness?" he demanded.

"I'd rely on my knowledge of science and common sense," I said.

"I'd trust in God," he countered. "For when Elijah was in the wilderness, God sent ravens to feed him. And he'd do the same for me if I trusted him."

"Well, it shouldn't be too hard to find out," I said.

I don't know why I said "science." I meant the kind of survival skills one learns in the Boy Scouts or the armed forces. The word science is a red flag to the Jesus people. Science connotes reason, and reason means sinful human nature in rebellion against God. As we left the rap, one of the kids immediately asked me if I believed in the theory of evolution. This was not the first time a Jesus freak had raised the issue. Before I went to California, I naïvely assumed that opposition to Darwinism belonged to the past, to the era of the Scopes Trial and the fundamentalist-modernist controversy. But the Jesus movement's rejection of modern culture runs much deeper than I had suspected. The fundamentalism of fifty years ago is alive and well and lives in the Jesus people. Except for their hip vernacular and the way they dress, it is almost as if the twentieth century had bypassed the Jesus people. Most of them wish it had.

Mary and Whale were at that rap. Talk about children of our time! Mary and Whale have been living together for three years. They have a plump ten-month-old son named Django. Whale was the biggest (literally and figuratively) speed dealer in San Francisco. He and his friends would manufacture a batch of speed, rush out and sell it on the street, spend all the money on heroin, rush back to their place, and mainline themselves into nirvana. "There's not a place in my entire body where I did not shoot smack," Mary told me. Mary has been on welfare and dope for nearly a decade. She has lost two children—lost them the way you or I would lose a coin which dropped out of a pocket unnoticed. And just before the end, just before the final ride to oblivion, Mary and Whale had enough; they decided to leave the nightmare world they had so long inhabited. And Mary found Jesus.

Whale is not a Christian. It was actually a relief to talk with him. "What do you think about all this?" I asked. "About Mary and all this." I motioned toward the Jesus people around us.

"I'll tell you one thing," Whale responded. "It's better than drugs. It's sure as hell better than drugs."

Now it is one matter when nice goody-goody professionals and clerics tell you, "At least these Jesus freaks aren't on drugs." But when the biggest speed dealer in San Francisco tells you, "It's better than drugs," man, you had better believe that it is better than drugs!

And you know something else? I am going to keep in touch with Mary and Whale. I want to know what her psychiatrist says about her conversion, and if there is any improvement in the condition of her drug-damaged brain, and how Whale makes out when he comes up for trial on an old possession rap, and whether the social worker allows Mary to visit her "lost" daughter Rebecca. Somehow their lives are of deep interest to me, and if the Jesus movement can help Mary and Whale, I want it to.

I have stated that the high percentage of former dopers among the Jesus people was a surprise to

Illustration from The Hollywood Free Paper

me. But I would like to add one observation lest
I convey the wrong impression. Although most of
the Jesus people I met had a history of drug use,
I would not jump to the conclusion that they were
addicts or entrenched members of the counter-culture before their conversions. There is a wide gap
between drug experimentation and drug depen-
dence. Jesus freaks tend to overstate their prior sins.
After all, the lower one sank before finding Jesus,
the more miraculous his or her transformation will
be regarded. In this way status is conferred. Arthur
Blessitt tells of one man, Louis McDonald, who had
been convicted of two murders before his conversion. After he was saved, he was passed from church
to church, from group to group, so that Christians
could marvel at the saving power of the gospel (and
vicariously enjoy his sins). "He was," notes Blessitt

"a showpiece being used to frighten children." As McDonald himself relates: "Those preachers and congregations wanted every grotesque detail, every ounce of sin. The more horrible I made my testimony, the more thrilled they were. It was like a hanging or a bullfight." [19]

McDonald was ashamed of his past and wanted to forget it, but many Jesus freaks wallow in their pre-Christian sins (often with a noticeable tinge of nostalgia). I was frequently introduced to someone in the following manner: "This is Brother Al. He used to shoot up a hundred and fifty dollars worth of smack before God busted him." Mary, who was an actual heroin addict for years, told me that much of this is sheer fiction. "These kids, talking about getting saved and never wanting dope again. It just isn't that way. When I gave up smack—wow! Every nerve in your body comes to life and you hurt everywhere. Every joint aches. You feel sick to your stomach. You retch. You moan. You scream. You can't eat or sleep or do anything but think of getting a fix. But these kids who say they quit cold turkey and felt great and never wanted another fix! They're either lying or they only shot smack once or twice."

Some groups may be ninety percent former heavy dopers, but many of them came across as former plastic hippies or weekend street people at best. The hip, "with it," youth-oriented lingo of the Jesus freaks gives the impression that all the Jesus people are redeemed hippies, street people, heads, radicals, etc. The standard uniform—long hair, beads, ponchos, beards, overalls, workshirts, and sandals—supports the image. But appearances can be deceiving. For every ex-junkie and former hippie there is a clean-scrubbed, rosy-cheeked, non-alienated "kid next door" who never turned on or "took off" with anything more potent than Mom's apple pie or necking at the neighborhood drive-in. Such kids may claim to be "love revolutionaries stoned on Jesus the liberator," who are no longer "hung up on materialism," who have "beat the system," who find Jesus "neat, a gas, out of sight,"

Poster
Courtesy The Hollywood Free Paper Emporium, *reproduced by permission.*
© *Copyright 1971*

who "groove on God, experience his life-style, and find a permanent high," but the thought persists in my mind that many of the Jesus people have been initiated into youth culture by the very movement which rejects that culture, that is, by the Jesus movement itself. Not every Jesus freak was a freak before his conversion. Freeman Rogers of the Children of God told me that he had been beaten on several occasions by irate parents who resented the fact that the movement had made freaks (in the old-fashioned sense of the word) out of their children. Perhaps these parents sensed the truth so well expressed by San Francisco's Eric Hoffer, "Absolute faith corrupts as absolutely as absolute power."

Surprises
and
Tears

Was everything among the Jesus freaks pretty much as I had expected?

No. My anticipations had been wrong in several respects.

The high percentage of ex-dopers was a real surprise to me. I had expected about ten percent former drug users and about ninety percent average, normal kids who were simply attracted to a reasonably harmless youth fad. What I found was ninety percent former addicts. I must have forgotten just how serious Middle America's drug problem has become.

A second unanticipated finding was the extent of Pentecostalism among the Jesus people. The leaders who receive the most attention from the press— Arthur Blessitt, Duane Pederson, and Jack Sparks— are all fundamentalist revivalists in the Billy Graham tradition. Most of them either ignore so-called manifestations of the Spirit—speaking in tongues, healing, prophetic utterance—or they are actively opposed to them. Hal Lindsey teaches that such gifts of grace were limited to the apostolic church and are no longer operative. Sparks is not so sure. But among the organized communal groups such as the Children of God, the Alamos' Christian Foundation, and Calvary Chapel's youth ministries, tongues are considered the only infallible proof of baptism by the Holy Spirit. And although salvation is one thing and possession of the Spirit quite another, without tongues a deep and fulfilling spiritual life is considered an impossibility.

Pentecostalism adds the further complication of Arminianism, the belief that a born-again Christian can lose his salvation by his postconversion sins. The Pentecostals of the Jesus movement reject the doctrine of eternal security, the once-saved-always-saved assurance entertained by most evangelical Christians. This is a sore point of contention between the Pentecostals and the non-Pentecostals. In the words of Hal Lindsey, "God's not an Indian giver. He knew what kind of stinker you were before he accepted you. When Jesus died on the cross, all my sins were in the future—all my sins, not only those I committed before I was saved." (Several Jesus people, including friends of Hal, suggested that he may have good reason for stressing this doctrine.) But Tony and Sue Alamo insist that God is a God of love only to those who do his will and a God of wrath to those who depart from his commandments. There is no question in my mind that the eternal security approach encourages a "revolving door" Christianity, an "easy believism" which tolerates actions that should be condemned and de-emphasizes the need for postconversion discipline. But the "do as you're told or go to hell" legalism of the Alamos and the Children of God leaves much to be desired. I remember too many Christians from Nazarene and primitive Methodist backgrounds who were literally driven insane by the fear that they had jeopardized their salvation by a single lustful thought or a careless action. It seems that the Jesus people will have to work out the legalism-or-license issue just as the early church had to.

A third surprise was the disembodied, physical up-tightness of the movement. After my exposure to the sensitivity training or encounter group scene with its "touch me, feel me, heal me" emphasis on physical contact as a means of expressing oneself, I was aghast at the "keep your hands to yourself" spirit of the Jesus people's praise and worship ser-

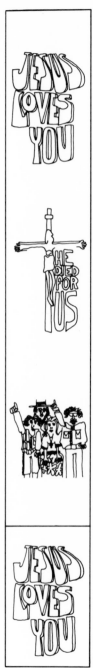

Cartoon from The Hollywood Free Paper

Courtesy of Adam's Apple—Hard Core, Ft. Wayne, Indiana

Jesus Rock Concert Ad

vices and their communal life. My temperament is so different. I hugged kids who were ecstatic with joy, placed an arm around a shoulder of a brother in anguish, stood toe-to-toe with my hands on the forearms of those I disagreed with, embraced new-found friends when I left them. But for the most part the Jesus people seem disgusted by physical contact. I do not wish to suggest a Freudian explanation even though I have never encountered such fear of human sexuality. (One brother put it thus: "All the girls in this group have three hymens.") However, I want to point out a kind of personal isolation, an acute estrangement from the emotions of other people and finally from one's own feelings, which follows from a Jesus-and-me spirituality which *excludes* rather than *includes* normal interpersonal relationships.

Finally, I must mention what I regard the greatest surprise—the sudden popularity of Jesus among our super-sophisticated young people. The Jesus movement has not been the only segment of today's young people to appropriate the figure of Jesus of Nazareth. There is at present a "Jesus fad" in popular culture. Its manifestations include the runaway popularity of the British rock opera *Jesus Christ Superstar,* the off-Broadway musical *Godspell,* the frequent appearance on the bestselling record charts of gospel songs ("Amazing Grace," "O Happy Day," and "Put Your Hand in the Hand") as well as quasi-gospel songs ("Let It Be," "Bridge over Troubled Waters," and "My Sweet Lord"—none of which proclaim the gospel of Jesus Christ but all of which assume a revival-hymn form). Typical of the new interest in religion of current popular culture is James Taylor, the first new star of the seventies, who asserts, "I think there's probably a God-shaped hole in everybody's being. Even if God only exists in people's minds, He's still a force. I believe in God, and I believe in Jesus, as a man, a metaphor and a phenomenon." [20] "To me Jesus is a metaphor, but also a manifestation of needs and feelings people have deep within themselves." [21]

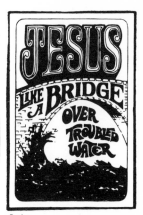

Poster
Courtesy The Hollywood Free Paper Emporium, *reproduced by permission.*
© Copyright 1971

In his finest song, "Fire and Rain," Taylor reaches beyond insanity and despair for the comfort of a savior.

But to Taylor as to many other rock poets, Jesus remains only "a metaphor . . . a manifestation of needs." Having turned previously for inspiration to drugs and oriental wisdom, and having discovered that drugs kill and mysticism confuses, the rock scene is now looking to something more familiar—to residual Christian themes. None of the new Jesus works proclaim the message of the Jesus freaks. Hence most of the Jesus people abhor them, regarding them as Satan's counterfeit gospel. Other Jesus freaks treat them sympathetically, as sincere expressions of their generation's hunger for the Lordship of Jesus.

Exactly who is the Jesus of the Jesus freaks? After all, virtually every major movement claims the inspiration of Jesus of Nazareth. There is a Marxist Jesus who condemns the establishment, a pacifistic Jesus who shuns violence and engages in passive resistance to evil, a conservative Jesus who renders unto Caesar the things that are Caesar's, a sentimental Jesus who invites little children to sit upon his lap, a man-of-action Jesus who chases the money-lenders from the temple precincts, a white Anglo-Saxon Jesus with blonde hair and blue eyes who sanctifies the superiority of pure Aryan stock, and the Semitic and dark-skinned Jesus who belongs to all oppressed peoples and exploited minorities. For throughout history Jesus has been interpreted by each age as the perfect man, the goal or exemplar which all men should strive to achieve. Thus, it should come as no surprise that the Jesus of the former hippies and ex-junkies is a man at odds with the establishment, a man who befriends the outcasts and dropouts, a man whose appearance and apparel are not only unanticipated but actually offensive to preconceptions of proper citizens and church members.

The Jesus people do not have a clear, consistent image of Jesus. They excel at feelings, not ideas—so

Photo courtesy of The Hollywood Free Paper, *Tom Jackson, staff photographer*

Gospel Rock Groups, The Dove Sounds

Photo by Jack Sparks

Larry Norman Sings

**GIVE·JESUS
A CHANCE**

**JESUS IS
MY BAG ✝**

**JESUS PEOPLE
UNITE!**

**JESUS ✝
IS COMING ✝**

Bumperstickers
Courtesy The Hollywood Free Paper
Emporium, reproduced by permission.
ⓒ *Copyright 1971*

it is not strange that they lack a developed chris-
tology. Jesus lives in their hearts. He has changed
their lives. He is a friend who listens to their problems
and tells them what to do by giving them the right
feeling at the right time. They have surrendered their
wills to his. Bad vibrations mean "don't." Good vibes
signal "that's cool—do it."

It is easier to determine what the Jesus of the
Jesus movement *is not* than what he *is.* He is not
the holier-than-thou, "get a haircut and get a job,
attend the right places with the right people and
you will get ahead" Jesus. Nor is he the "do whatever you want to and I will always love and understand
you no matter what" Jesus. He is the friend who
accepts you regardless of the past but who expects
you to shape up or else.

What bothers me is that the Jesus movement
Christ is a "sacrifice your personality to the control
of your superego" version of the "real" Jesus. For
the typical Jesus freak is someone who could not
handle his freedom prior to his conversion, someone
who could not wisely use all the possibilities available to him. So rather than continue to risk disaster,
rather than play around with such dangerous forces
as drugs, sex, and violence, he surrenders his will
to the internalized prohibitions which all of us carry
around inside of us as the result of our family training
and social pressures. Thus the Jesus freak makes
peace with an uneasy conscience. But not only is
the Jesus movement version of Jesus a strict internal
monitor who floods us with anxieties if we as much
as contemplate forbidden actions, but he is a remor-
seless censor as well—a censor who allows no
imagination or independence.

Let's face it. The Jesus freaks have few ideas
about anything. Their conversation, art, and literature is cliché-ridden from beginning to end. They
are more like beavers duplicating the perfect dams
of older beavers than creative, adventerous human
beings. The Jesus freak knows where his independence got him in the past. He is too afraid that he
may lose the comfort, security, and self-acceptance

which he has gained. To think for oneself, to question and criticize, to seek fresh explanations of the mysteries of faith—such undertakings are to hazardous to be encouraged either by the individual or the group. For the only way that self-dissatisfaction may be conquered is by submerging one's individuality in the community of Jesus-obeying disciples. As a sign in the kitchen at the Children of God headquarters proclaims: *"There is no room for self here."*

No room for self. No room for individual insight or personal perspective. No room for fantasy or inventiveness. No room for the rich store of individual or collective unconsciousness. No room for self.

A presidential election is about to be held. A constitutional amendment has given the vote to men and women as young as eighteen. By the time America goes to the voting booths, hundreds of thousands of newly enfranchised citizens will be converts to the Jesus people. In fact, I expect the Jesus movement to be *the* youth fad for the next eighteen months. And how will they vote? Will the Jesus people support hawks or doves, conservatives or liberals, integrationists or segregationists, internationalists or neo-isolationists? *The saddest thing that I will say in this book is that they probably will not vote at all.* A huge portion of the new electorate will simply be neutralized by the Jesus movement. For there is no room in the movement for the discussion of politics, international or local issues, the salvation of the environment, or the resurrection of the cities. During the next year and a half the Jesus people will be too busy discussing the Bible, proclaiming the salvation of souls, the resurrection of Jesus, and the impending end of the world to care who is elected to the presidency or the Congress of the United States of America. Is it any wonder that the New Left considers the Jesus movement a conspiracy sponsored by right-wing money to pacify American youth in order to preserve the *status quo?*

Unless a religious issue materializes in the next

Poster
Courtesy The Hollywood Free Paper Emporium, *reproduced by permission.*
© *Copyright 1971*

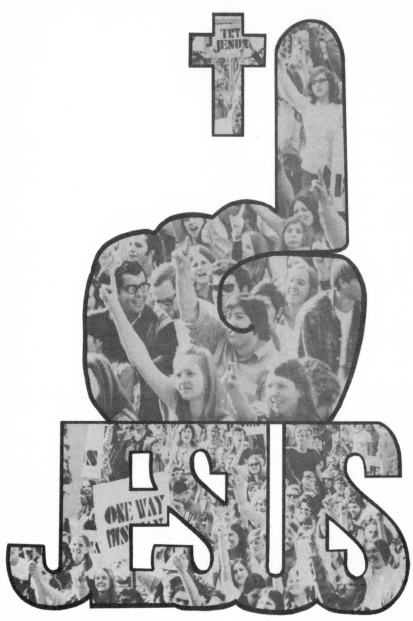

Poster

Courtesy The Hollywood Free Paper Emporium,
reproduced by permission.
© Copyright 1971

few months, an issue such as the Roman Catholic faith of John F. Kennedy in 1960, the Jesus freaks will totally ignore the election. There is always the possibility that an unscrupulous politican may inject religion into the forthcoming campaign, may attempt to package himself as a "Bible-believing, born-again Christian," may appeal to his friendship with Billy Graham, may even declare that his opponent does not believe in God, Jesus, or the American way. Only in this way can the Jesus freaks be attracted to the most basic duty of citizenship in a democracy, the right to vote.

Does God so detest his creatures that in order to please him they must sacrifice all that makes each distinct from the others, must think alike, act alike, dress alike, use the same limited supply of slogans and clichés? It was because I believed that God loved me that I learned to love myself. And because I could accept myself I came to desire the fulfillment of my unique potential as a person. And so I ask each Jesus freak, What does Jesus require? The flowering of your distinctiveness or the destruction of your individuality?

Bumpersticker
Courtesy The Hollywood Free Paper Emporium, *reproduced by permission.*
© *Copyright 1971*

What
of
Tomorrow?

What of tomorrow? Will the movement run out of
hippies, dopers, bikers, runaways, and the other
social castoffs it has been attracting? Even if the
supply of street people is limitless, I have seen a
gradual change occurring. More and more of the
new arrivals are middle class kids who have never
opted out of straight society. Some of them have
been fundamentalists for years, others are new converts who still value middle class existence and look
forward to a productive career, a good marriage,
and a happy family. They are anxious to find emotional satisfaction through the most involving movement around—the Jesus movement. But they do not
wish to give up the world of everyday life. Lately
there are huge numbers of teeny-bopper Christians
eager to be "where it's at," to get in on the action.
Their symbol should be a plastic statuette of Jesus,
for these are the plastic Jesus people. And with the
teeny-boppers come the commercializers—the recording companies, the movie studios (I can see
it now—"The Jesus Freaks Meet the Son of Fran-
kenstein in the Valley of the Dolls," starring Pat
Boone as Arthur Blessitt), the souvenir hawkers, and
the press agents. Finally, there have arrived the
"false prophets." Some self-appointed leaders en-
courage the new-born Christians to accept with
thanksgiving all that God has created (including
drugs and illicit sex). Such Christian libertines are

already active in southern California. Others order Christians to flee from their friends, homes, and families so that they may seek refuge in the Midwest from the cataclysm which will soon engulf the Pacific Coast. Everywhere private revelations are being received.

What will happen to the Jesus freaks? Will the movement fragment into a hundred sects, each of which clings to a divinely inspired leader? Will the youthful zeal of the Jesus people diminish as they are forced to deal with daily problems in a world that stubbornly refuses to come to an end? Will they marry, raise families, and wander into the established denominational and fundamentalist churches? Or will totally new forms of Christian institutions emerge? Perhaps the Christian commune or family of families will replace the chapel on the street corner. Perhaps small groups of Christian couples meeting in homes on weekday evenings to discuss common problems, to read the Bible, and to pray for one another will flourish while the mainline denominations wither away through public ne-

Photo courtesy of The Hollywood Free Paper, *Tom Jackson, staff photographer*

Bible Rap at The Hollywood Free Paper

glect. Perhaps the hundreds of small Jesus movement groups will discover that the really hard work
of being a Christian comes after conversion for both
the convert and the convert-maker. Perhaps the
Jesus freaks will learn that even if every man,
woman, and child were to accept Christ, the task
of solving America's social, political, moral, and
ecological problems would only have begun. Only
time will tell.

"Youth is a wonderful thing," a wise man once
mused. "What a pity that it's wasted on the young."
In a few years will we ruefully add, "Christianity is
a wonderful thing. What a pity it was wasted on the
Jesus freaks"?

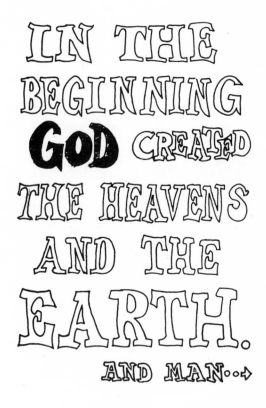

A
Personal
Postlude

I was in Sherman Oaks, a Los Angeles suburb,
the house guest of Bill and Dottie Fitzgerald, friends
of my parents. They introduced me to Mary Anne,
their neighbor. Mary Anne is thirty, divorced, and
has two young daughters, Amber and Beth. (Before
I met Mary Anne, I had spent an afternoon in the
Fitzgeralds' swimming pool, entertaining her girls
and my host's son and daughter.) Mary Anne is an
unordained lady preacher who prays in tongues and
casts demons out of Christians (translation: she
frees them from such "errors" as psychiatry, astrology, meditation, and spiritualism—all of which have
hundreds of thousands of devotees in Los Angeles).

As we talked, Mary Anne put me through the usual
catechism that I had come to expect from Pentecostals in the Jesus movement:

Mary Anne: Are you saved?

Me: Yes.

Mary Anne: You're Jewish aren't you?

Me: Do I look Jewish?

Mary Anne: Yes.

Me: Well, I am Jewish, but I've been a Christian
for seventeen years.

Mary Anne: Praise the Lord! The Lord is calling
his people unto himself in these last days. (Pause.)
Have you received the Spirit?

Me: Yes.

Mary Anne: Do you have "tongues"?

Me: No. That's not my gift. I'm not against tongues.

I've never decided not to speak in tongues. It's just that it's never happened to me.

We talked for an hour or so about our families, about our personal religious experiences, about studying the Bible. As I was about to leave, Mary Anne asked if she could pray with me. I consented. She began in tongues, gibberish to me which sounded like phrases from Hebrew and Spanish. Then she asked God to unbind me, to help me realize that I am his child and heir, not a beggar but a child and heir. Now my interpretation of my needs is far different than Mary Anne's. But I was deeply touched that she cared to pray for me, for the whole time I was with the Jesus people, no one else did. And that is wierd. When I passed through *my* Jesus freak stage, all of us born-again teen-agers prayed together on every conceivable occasion. We cared. And we did more than pray. If we could, we helped. I will always remember the time shortly before our daughter was born when I found myself between jobs. Two college girls whom we had known in Chicago sent us ten dollars. Here was a negotiable "God bless you."

Three days after my conversation with Mary Anne it was Father's Day, and I was three thousand miles away from my own children. The three handmade cards—two from seven-year-old Tara Fitzgerald and one from Amber—meant much to me. Amber's card featured a gold-star-spangled cover, a touching poem, and a personal note:

Dear Lole,

I hope you have a very, very nice Father's Day! I like you so very much, and you are so sweet and fun. May God bless always! I hope you live a happy, happy life and a peaceful one too! And let there be a joyful song in your heart forever, and may the Lord keep you always.

Lord bless you with love,
Amber

P.S. I love you!

Poster
Courtesy The Hollywood Free Paper Emporium, *reproduced by permission.*
© *Copyright 1971*

Poster

"Jesus is alive!" proclaims a poster before me which I picked up at the *Hollywood Free Paper.* If he is, he lives in the Ambers of this world.

On my last night in Berkeley I went to church with Mary and the Ortegas. Mary had invited us. She is part of the "Christian Fellowship, Berkeley," a small group which meets in the chapel of Trinity Methodist Church. Nothing that happens in this fellowship will attract the attention of *Time, Life,* or *Newsweek.* A quiet, dull, straight sermon on temptation was given by a long-haired, bearded young man in a neatly pressed brown suit, white shirt, narrow tie, and shined shoes. "Lack of faith is the greatest sin," he declared. "You can go to hell for lack of faith. If you don't believe, you're not saved." A pianist, guitarist, and violinist—all of high school age—accompanied the congregational singing. It was all very quiet, very mellow, very peaceful. As we sang "Near the Cross" and "Amazing Grace," two of the young men began dancing before the altar. It was intimate; it was joyous; it was real.

And I wept.

Yes. I wept.

First for myself. For seventeen years of lessons. For the realization that the burden is heavy and the way is hard.

Then for my brothers and sisters, babes in Christ, lambs among jackals, the blind led by the blind, sheep with no shepherd.

Next for my world and my generation. For if that world is not coming to an end, maybe it should.

And finally for my son and daughter. For if I could, I would give them a better world. But I cannot. So I despair. And I walk with them a long, long road that leads, I pray, to the city of our God.

Button
Courtesy The Hollywood Free Paper Emporium, *reproduced by permission.*
© *Copyright 1971*

Notes

[1] Duane Pederson, *Jesus People* (Pasadena, California: Compass Press, 1971), p. 35.

[2] Arthur Blessitt, *Turned on to Jesus* (New York: Hawthorn Books, 1971), p. 1.

[3] Pederson, *Jesus People*, p. 35.

[4] "News and Views" section, July 4, 1971.

[5] The venerable King James Version is the only translation permitted by the Alamos and the Children of God. Duane Pederson promotes a fundamentalist version known as the King James II Bible. The college-oriented groups such as the JC Light and Power House rely on the recent American Standard Version, produced by a covey of conservative Protestants as an alternative to the Revised Standard Version. Jack Sparks pushes both the Kenneth N. Taylor paraphrase distributed by the Billy Graham Evangelistic Association *(Living Letters)* and his own "Street Christian" version. Some kids prefer the sophomoric *Amplified New Testament.* Totally ignored are such excellent translations as the Revised Standard Version, J. B. Phillips' New Testament, and the American Bible Society's *Good News for Modern Man.*

[6] *Hollywood Free Paper,* June 15, 1971, p. 2.

[7] Bryan Wilson, *Religious Sects* (New York: McGraw-Hill, 1970), p. 49.

[8] Edward John Carnell, *The Case for Orthodox Theology* (Philadelphia: Westminster Press, 1959), p. 113.

[9] L. Harold DeWolf, *Present Trends in Christian Thought* (Reflection Books; New York: Association Press, 1960), pp. 47-49.

[10] *Ibid.,* p. 50.

[11] Jerald C. Brauer, *Protestantism in America* (Philadelphia: Westminster Press, 1965), pp. 216-17.

[12] Edward John Carnell, "Fundamentalism," *A Handbook of Christian Theology* (New York: Living Age Books, 1958), pp. 142-43.

[13] Thomas F. O'Dea, *The Sociology of Religion* (Englewood Cliffs, N.J.: Prentice-Hall, 1966), p. 69. See also H. Richard Niebuhr, *The Social Sources of Denominationalism* (New York: Henry Holt & Co., 1929).

127

[14] Allan H. Sager, "The Fundamentalist-Modernist Controversy, 1918-1930," *Preaching in American History*, ed. DeWitte Holland (Nashville: Abingdon Press, 1969), p. 272.

[15] Wilson, *Religious Sects*, p. 94.

[16] Robert Paul Wolff, review of Lewis S. Feuer, *The Conflict of Generations*, in *The New York Times Book Review*, March 30, 1969, p. 32.

[17] Kenneth Keniston, *The Uncommitted: Alienated Youth in American Society* (New York: Harcourt, Brace & World, 1965), p. 398.

[18] Theodor Reik, *Of Love and Lust* (New York: Bantam Books, 1967), pp. 130-31.

[19] Blessitt, *Turned on to Jesus*, p. 89.

[20] Quoted by Susan Braudy, "James Taylor, a New Troubadour," *The New York Times Magazine*, February 21, 1971, p. 88.

[21] "The New Rock: Bittersweet and Low," *Time*, March 1, 1971, p. 49.